Way of the Cyber Warrior:

Ageless Wisdom to Build a Strong Security Mindset

Corey M. Hubbert

PUBLISHED BY: Corey M. Hubbert

Copyright©2024 All rights reserved.

No part of this publication may be copied or reproduced in any format, by any means, electronic or otherwise, without prior written consent from the copyright owner and publisher of this book.

Table of Contents

About the Author i

How to use this book. iv

Foreword vi

Introduction viii

"If you know the way broadly, you will see it in everything." viii

One must make the warrior walk his everyday walk. 1

The body and soul of a tactician must always be prepared for battle. If one is unprepared, one is certainly on the way to defeat. 4

Deliberate often – Decide once. 6

Man is only as strong as his convictions and beliefs. 8

Do not seek to follow in the footsteps of wise men; seek what they sought. 10

To know and to act are one and the same. 12

We make war that we may live in peace. 14

The wise man hides his weapons. 17

Carelessness is a great enemy. 19

To spare the ravening leopard is an act of injustice to the sheep. 22

The best armor is to keep out of range. 25

What is of supreme importance in war is to attack the enemy's strategy. 27

Reputation often spills less blood. 30

Rely not on the likelihood of the enemy's not coming, but on our own readiness to receive him; not on the chance of his not attacking, but rather on the fact that we have made our position unassailable. 33

Do not be tricked into thinking that there are no crocodiles just because the water is still. 36

You must be deadly serious in training. 39

He is victorious who knows when and when not to fight. 41

Focus on your one purpose. 43

Tomorrow's battle is won during today's practice..................46

The bird that offers itself to the net is fair game to the fowler. 49

Freedom is the only worthy goal in life. It is won by disregarding things that lie beyond our control. 52

Though we are powerful and strong, and we know how to fight, we do not wish to fight...55

By keeping your weapons in order, your enemy will be subjugated. 58

The path of the warrior is lifelong, and mastery is often simply staying on the path. 61

Think, feel, and act like a warrior. Set yourself apart from the rest of society by your personal excellence...........................64

The wise hawk conceals his talons. 67

In order to progress in life, one has to improve every day in an endless process..70

Take away the cause, and the effect ceases............................74

It is no honor for an eagle to vanquish a dove. 77

Noblemen discipline themselves to be dignified at all times... Sharpen your mind and show your dignity...........................80

To be prepared for war is one of the most effective means of preserving peace..83

To subdue an enemy without fighting is the greatest of skills. 86

To see is to be deceived, to feel is to know. 89

Make yourself a sheep, and the wolf is ready. 92

A man who has attained mastery of an art reveals it in his every action. 95

The important thing is to be always moving forward, little by little. 98

The just man is not one who does harm to none, but one whom having the power to harm represses the will. 101

The true warrior ponders the future without discarding the past while living in the present. 104

Trained fighters, much more than average people, have an obligation to employ their skills judiciously. To govern themselves and their emotions at all times..........................107

The first law of war is to preserve ourselves and destroy the enemy..111

The more you sweat in training, the less you bleed in battle. 114

But here we may wonder what he would do if nobody knew anything about it. 117

The angry man will defeat himself in battle as in life. 119

In God we trust, the rest we polygraph. 122

Anger breeds confusion. To be clear-minded, you must avoid being angry. 125

Look well into thyself; there is a source of strength which will always spring up if thou wilt always look......................128

Do, or do not. There is no try. 131

There is a best way to perform any task. 134

A man's word is his honor. 137
Don't appear just; be just. 140

About the Author

In a world where technology is taking over, conflict has moved from real-world settings into virtual ones. In the field of cybersecurity, where battles are waged on a regular basis against invisible foes, the same ideas that lead warriors in warfare have found new importance. I have worked at the nexus of these two worlds for my entire career, and it is an honor to impart the knowledge I have learned from them into this book.

Thirty years ago, I began this path as a computer network engineer. Here, I first developed a thorough understanding of the digital infrastructure that supports our modern world. During this period, my adventures in the cybersecurity domain began. The power of cyber warfare to cripple economies and governments soon became the leading influencer in my bid to join the FBI.

For the last twenty years of my life, as an FBI special agent, I have devoted my energy to investigating complex cybercrimes and conducting sophisticated technical operations to gather evidence to help prosecute criminal activity. As an FBI Unit Chief in the Operational Technology Division (OTD), I had the privilege of overseeing the bureau's offensive and defensive technical surveillance operations programs.

Complimenting these positions, I have been a practitioner of Jiu-Jujitsu for over 20 years, a discipline that has taught me resilience, adaptability, and strategic thinking—skills I have been able to teach other agents as an FBI defensive tactics instructor.

As an adjunct faculty member in the FBI's Cyber Division, I have and continue to pass on my Cyber expertise to the upcoming generation of FBI cyber warriors. This book is a culmination of thirty years of work in the digital realm and sphere of warrior strategic thinking.

This book seeks to provide the tools and foundational knowledge to those navigating the dangerous seas of cybersecurity, cyber warfare, and beyond. The motivation for this book stems from my career as a Special Agent, my black belt in Jiu Jitsu, and my expertise in cybersecurity. These experiences have enabled me to thwart cyber-attacks effectively and honorably. It is easy to approach battles with anger and a desire for revenge, but doing so only perpetuates the endless cycle of hate, fear, and conflict.

I have chosen to embed all this knowledge in the context of ancient warrior wisdom, as their approach to battle and warfare, regardless of the medium, has proven timeless. Their truths offer valuable insights into today's contemporary challenges.

In this book, I will explore the remarkable similarities between traditional warrior wisdom and contemporary cybersecurity techniques. In doing so, I hope to achieve a piece of work that will provide the reader with the tools to be a true warrior with a high moral code in a chaotic world reminiscent of the Wild West. Every warrior code will serve to elevate your professional and personal development to enhance your cyber defenses, as well as your personal life.

As with the way of the warrior, this journey is a lifetime endeavor, for mastery consists of continuing the path even when confronted with struggle.

-Corey M. Hubbert

How to use this book.

Warrior wisdom, which has been passed down through the years, can help you not only in martial arts but also in your personal and professional lives. To use this knowledge, you need a strategy. As the ancient saying goes, "Seek the past to find the future."

Here's how to put these lessons into practice in your daily life:

1. Although the wisdom in this book is short, they are deep in meaning. You might be inclined to read in one sitting, but that would be a mistake. Doing so could lead to a lack of understanding. Take your time, ponder, and meditate on each wisdom. Reflect on the principles and give them time to sink in so you can fully grasp their significance. Read with an open mind and an open heart.

2. After reading a particular piece of warrior wisdom, take some time to think about the meaning. Reflect on what it teaches and, most importantly, how it relates to your life. Consider how it could help you with the challenges you face at home and in your career. This kind of self-reflection will

help the principles become part of you and your new journey, guiding your actions and choices.

3. *Way of the Cyber Warrior* is a journey of self-improvement and professional mastery. As you grow and encounter new challenges, you might find that revisiting this book and its wisdom will keep you focused. By doing so, you will ensure that these messages remain in your thoughts, continue to aid your growth, and deepen your understanding.

Warrior wisdoms are more than just phrases and maxims. They are guiding principles that, when applied properly, can significantly impact one's personal and professional life. The key is to approach them with an open mind, a reflective spirit, and a willingness to apply and reapply their lessons as you navigate the changing landscapes of life and career.

Foreword

Written by Sheena Patel, author of *Yoga: Where the Impossible Meets the Possible"* and founder of Ancient Yoga School

As a human living the life of a Yogi for the last 20 years, I find this book profoundly refreshing in a working world largely devoid of compassion and a moral compass. As humans, we often seek change in our lives but rarely in how we conduct our work. Given the current business practices and their influence over our lives, it is imperative that change extends into the economic sphere, especially since economics contribute to the chaos presently afflicting our world.

As more of our lives are uploaded into the digital world, cybersecurity has become more relevant than ever before. It is crucial that we establish a foundation for how this digital world will be orchestrated by those who conduct it. After all, it is the conductors who set the tone.

This book's importance lies in its understanding that to keep us safe, we must approach this sector as warriors once approached life and war—with awareness, compassion, thought, and a strong ethical and moral code. Learning to respond to threats rather than react to them is essential.

Such qualities can only arise from within the individual rather than through a set of work guidelines. This book provides all the tools needed to create change in those who step into the cyber realm so they may lead in how this new world unfolds. The goal is to create not only a safer world but a better, more enlightened one, where we guide the digital rather than allowing the digital to guide us.

This is a book for those seeking to lead, create change, and become modern-day warriors in a world greatly lacking the ancient codes that once gave rise to a more informed society. It is not just for professionals but anyone who has uploaded a part of their life into the cyber world.

Corey encapsulates and lives by every word laid down on these pages in both his personal and professional life. His professional life spans the private sector and his twenty years in the FBI, while his personal life has been influenced by the code of the Jiu-Jitsu warrior. As a black belt, he has been teaching this code to law enforcement for over fifteen years.

As such, he is a pivotal figure in defining how we move forward into a cyber world that presently resembles the Wild West. This book, on every page, reminds us to be ethical warriors rather than reactive villains.

Introduction

"If you know the way broadly, you will see it in everything."

-Miyamoto Musashi

The true warrior is an uncommon individual in today's world, which often prioritizes convenience over integrity and shortcuts over prolonged effort. The warrior's way of life involves more than just strength and battle proficiency; it entails a steadfast dedication to a set of moral principles that cannot be compromised or wavered. Values such as honor, integrity, and doing what is right form the foundation of this way of life.

While martial arts and the art of self-defense are crucial parts of the journey, they are only a small part of the warrior's path. It is a holistic way of living that includes not only honing physical skills but also pursuing inner development. This way of thinking is similar to the Japanese concept of kaizen, which emphasizes continuous, unending improvement.

At the heart of the warrior lifestyle is a constant commitment to character development. True warriors strive to balance and elevate their spirit, mind, and body, much like the relentless pursuit of kaizen. Each of these three dimensions plays a unique role in creating the holistic warrior, making it essential to maintain their equal balance.

Training and martial arts proficiency are vital components of a warrior's path because they enhance preparedness and resilience. However, the warrior knows that character development is the cornerstone of their journey. This understanding emphasizes the commitment to developing not only physical prowess but also a firm moral compass.

Those who desire a life of excellence and discipline—a life guided by a strong code of ethics—are drawn to the warrior lifestyle. It is governed by a firm decision to uphold the values of honor, readiness, and righteousness rather than mere lip service. To walk the path of a warrior means to put morality above ease and to defend what is right over what is profitable. It necessitates dedication to one's family, friends, and the less fortunate. As the warrior carves out their individual place in the world, independence of thought and action becomes second nature.

The warrior's decision transcends cultural conventions and necessitates devotion to a higher standard; it is not restricted to a particular bloodline or origin. Anyone who aspires to live a life of respect and dignity and who wants to rise above the average is invited to adopt this way of life. It challenges people to embrace the road of discipline and perseverance rather than succumbing to the allure of shortcuts.

As you read the pages that follow, you will discover the essence of the warrior lifestyle. This way of life requires unshakable dedication, continuous growth, and the bravery to stand up for what is right. You will learn how to meet the challenges of the modern world while upholding the enduring values that form the basis of the warrior's code. May your journey through this book inspire you to live a life of honor, greatness, and significance, truly deserving of a warrior's legacy.

One must make the warrior walk his everyday walk.

Miyamoto Musashi

The ageless advice of Miyamoto Musashi, "One must make the warrior walk their everyday walk," resonates deeply with people and exhorts them to adopt the warrior mindset in all facets of life, not only during difficult times. This idea is especially applicable in modern settings like cybersecurity, where ongoing awareness is crucial to fending off evolving threats.

Fundamentally, Musashi's instruction emphasizes incorporating warrior ideals into everyday activities. This calls for cybersecurity professionals to embrace a constant state of preparedness and alertness, understanding that risks are always present in the digital sphere, no matter where they are or when they occur.

This attitude places a strong emphasis on the pursuit of lifelong learning and personal development. Like Musashi's commitment to mastering the art of the sword, cybersecurity specialists need to stay current with the latest developments in threats, technologies, and vulnerabilities. This lifelong learning process must include attending industry events, staying updated on training, and engaging with the cybersecurity community.

Furthermore, proactive defense tactics align with Musashi's focus on readiness. Just as a warrior must predict the movements of his enemies, cybersecurity experts must proactively strengthen systems against potential intrusions. This entails implementing strong defenses, conducting regular risk analyses, and staying vigilant for emerging threats.

The process of "making the warrior walk their everyday walk" in cybersecurity also requires the development of mental resilience. Professionals frequently work in stressful environments, so developing focus, tolerance, and adaptability is essential to overcoming obstacles.

Ethical behavior is equally essential in cybersecurity and forms a fundamental part of Musashi's philosophy. Cybersecurity professionals must adhere to the highest standards of integrity, protecting privacy and preserving stakeholder trust, given the sensitive nature of the data entrusted to them.

Overall, Musashi's maxim is a powerful reminder of the enduring relevance of warrior virtues in the digital age. By embodying the ideals of lifelong learning, proactive defense, mental resilience, and ethical conduct, cybersecurity professionals uphold the tradition of the warrior, safeguarding against modern threats and maintaining the integrity of digital landscapes.

The body and soul of a tactician must always be prepared for battle. If one is unprepared, one is certainly on the way to defeat.

Kazumi Tabata

Kazumi Tabata's profound statement encapsulates the essence of readiness for a tactician's success. It emphasizes the constant necessity for a tactician's body and mind to be prepared for battle, cautioning that failure to do so will inevitably result in defeat.

Tabata's observation highlights the critical importance of being ready on all fronts and draws attention to the intricate relationship between physical and mental preparedness. It implies that success hinges on having the mental and physical capacity to face challenges and make calculated decisions.

Viewed through the lens of a warrior, this guidance aligns with the concept of holistic readiness and the interdependence of body and mind. Warriors understand that being at the top of their physical and mental game is essential to winning battles.

To apply this notion to their field, consider a cybersecurity specialist who actively develops both technical skill and mental toughness. By combining academic knowledge with real-world experience, they effectively manage stress while staying up to date on the latest cyber threats and technologies, ensuring they are well-prepared to handle high-stakes cyber incidents.

This cybersecurity scenario further illustrates that cultivating a tactician's mental and physical well-being is crucial for success. Cybersecurity experts agree that total readiness—both physical and psychological—enhances their ability to respond efficiently and achieve targeted goals, much as Tabata warns of failure stemming from lack of preparation.

Ultimately, these pearls of wisdom serve as a sobering reminder of the critical importance of preparedness. Whether in personal development or career endeavors such as cybersecurity, remaining physically and psychologically ready is essential for overcoming obstacles and emerging victorious.

Deliberate often – Decide once.

Latin Proverb

The age-old maxim "Deliberate often – Decide once" captures the importance of giving decisions significant thought before making them. It preaches the benefits of careful consideration, patience, and a thorough analysis of all available options—values still applicable today, particularly in the quick-paced world of technology.

Every choice you make in the world of cybersecurity, where there are many hazards and high stakes, has a significant impact. This proverb is a painful reminder to those working in this industry to stop, think, and carefully consider all relevant information before moving forward.

Consider the introduction of new security technologies into an organization. Even though there may be pressure to implement quickly, especially in response to perceived threats, it is crucial to carefully consider the technology's functionality, design, and potential risks. Ensuring a well-founded and informed decision requires extensive testing, consulting with experts, and performing in-depth assessments.

Similarly, in the case of a security breach, it might be tempting to act swiftly. However, it is prudent to first determine the extent of the breach, pinpoint its source, and evaluate its impact to determine the best course of action. Making hasty decisions without thorough consideration could exacerbate the situation by creating additional vulnerabilities and problems.

This proverb is a helpful reminder of the enduring value of thoughtful decision-making in a society that often prioritizes quick fixes. In cybersecurity, as in life, well-thought-out, patient, and empathetic decisions are more likely to withstand the test of time and adversity.

Man is only as strong as his convictions and beliefs.

Kensho Furuya

The significant statement made by Kensho Furuya, "Man is only as strong as his convictions and beliefs," highlights the critical importance of moral and ethical values and provides a profound insight into the nature of strength. This is especially true in the field of cybersecurity, where ethical norms and personal beliefs have a significant impact on professional behavior and efficacy.

Furuya's comment encourages a closer examination of the fundamental ideas that govern practitioners' activities, even though technical expertise in cybersecurity frequently earns acclaim. In fact, a cybersecurity expert's moral compass ensures that their expertise is applied responsibly and ethically. Their views on privacy, security, and ethical duty significantly impact how they approach their profession.

Strong security measures are essential because of a firm commitment to protecting user data. Cybersecurity experts are motivated by their strong beliefs to take preventative measures, foresee new attacks, and fix possible weaknesses. Their tenacity and commitment are rooted in a deep conviction in the importance of their work, especially in the face of difficult security situations.

Furthermore, Furuya's observation emphasizes how crucial integrity is in the field of cybersecurity. In a setting where sensitive data is omnipresent, one's moral principles directly impact the adherence to ethical standards, ensuring user trust is maintained, and data is handled responsibly.

Moreover, advocacy and education are integral parts of a person's commitment to cybersecurity values. Enthusiastic professionals are essential in bringing attention to digital security and privacy issues, motivating others to prioritize these concerns, and fostering a cybersecurity-conscious culture within societies and businesses.

Essentially, Kensho Furuya's statement highlights that strength in cybersecurity is multidimensional, involving not only technological expertise but also a strong commitment to moral values. It suggests that true strength in this area arises from a dedication to upholding information security and ethical behavior rather than just technical skills. In an ever-digitizing environment, such a comprehensive viewpoint is essential for the diligent and successful practice of cybersecurity.

Do not seek to follow in the footsteps of wise men; seek what they sought.

Basho

The classic quotation from Basho, "Do not seek to follow in the footsteps of wise men, seek what they sought," captures the spirit of wisdom and encourages pursuing the underlying ambitions and aims rather than merely copying others. This wisdom emphasizes the value of exploring the fundamental goals and motivations that inspire wise people, emphasizing the pursuit of enlightenment more than shallow imitation.

Essentially, this quotation exhorts people to understand the meaning of wisdom, trying to absorb the values and concepts that underpin prudent behavior instead of simply copying acts. It is consistent with the strategic thinking tenets of a warrior's mindset, stressing the need to comprehend the fundamental ideas that guide successful endeavors.

Applying this knowledge to the field of cybersecurity, budding experts are encouraged to go beyond simply replicating seasoned specialists. Instead, they should analyze the processes, problem-solving strategies, and guiding principles that contribute to their success. By understanding the genuine goals and tactics these experts employ, aspiring professionals can innovate and adapt to the constantly changing threat landscape.

This cybersecurity case study highlights the benefit of learning from the pursuits of experienced individuals rather than copying them verbatim. Similar to Basho's advocacy for comprehension over mere imitation, prospective cybersecurity professionals gain knowledge that empowers them to navigate and innovate within an ever-evolving threat landscape.

In the end, Basho's counsel emphasizes the importance of understanding the intentions and motivations behind actions, advocating for a more profound comprehension that fosters genuine advancement and development. Seeking what wise individuals sought leads to deeper understanding and significant improvement, whether in professional or personal endeavors such as cybersecurity.

To know and to act are one and the same.

Samurai Maxim

The ancient Samurai saying, "To know and to act are one and the same," encapsulates a fundamental truth that has withstood the test of time and remains relevant in today's technologically advanced culture. This principle underscores the intimate connection between understanding and putting a topic into meaningful action.

Reflecting on the myriad policies, processes, and best practices available, one can draw comparisons to the complex realm of cybersecurity. The real challenge lies in implementation. While many organizations may be aware of these practices, actual effectiveness is determined by how well they are executed. For example, understanding the importance of encrypting sensitive data is one thing, but a business is truly protected only when all critical data is securely encrypted.

Modern cybersecurity experts must adopt a warrior mentality, ensuring that the principles they uphold are not just documented but deeply ingrained in the company's daily operations and culture, much like the Samurai did. Merely acknowledging the need for periodic system updates or two-factor authentication, for example, can lead to vulnerabilities, much as a superficial commitment to a Samurai's code could lead to downfall.

The Samurai viewed their principles as a way of life, not just a set of rules. Similarly, cybersecurity rules and recommendations should become deeply ingrained behaviors rather than mere checklists. Achieving true security requires dedication and consistency in applying these well-established principles.

The Samurai's age-old wisdom offers a timeless lesson. The meticulous procedures of a cybersecurity expert or the disciplined life of a warrior both require perfect information integration and continuous action. By actively studying and practicing what we know, we uphold the values of the Samurai and enhance our defenses in the digital age.

We make war that we may live in peace.

Aristotle

The age-old proverb attributed to Aristotle, "We make war that we may live in peace," captures the notion that temporary strife can lead to lasting peace and stability. This idea underscores the importance of taking preventive action, such as confronting threats when necessary, to maintain a safe and tranquil existence. However, given the dynamic nature of cybersecurity and the need to protect against malevolent actors, this idea calls for a nuanced approach because digital threats are constantly evolving.

In the context of cybersecurity, preventive defense and the proverb "prevention is better than cure" are intrinsically linked. Just as states work to ward off potential enemies and preserve peace, individuals and organizations engage in cybersecurity measures to prevent attacks and maintain the integrity of their digital ecosystems.

Consider a company that employs sophisticated threat detection systems, conducts regular security audits, trains its staff, and enforces robust cybersecurity protocols. These proactive initiatives require time, money, and technological resources. However, they enhance the company's ability to secure private information, maintain uninterrupted business operations, and protect sensitive data.

Similarly, cybersecurity experts take a proactive approach by continuously monitoring for vulnerabilities, anticipating potential attack vectors, and promptly addressing any identified weaknesses. Even in the face of attackers seeking to exploit flaws, these professionals adhere to Aristotle's advice by proactively and diligently reducing risks and creating a secure online environment.

While Aristotle's advice originally focused on interstate relations, its fundamental principles are applicable to cybersecurity. The pursuit of proactive defense reflects the overarching goal of achieving peace through deliberate action, embodying the idea that preparedness and strategic measures lead to a more secure and stable environment.

Incorporating Aristotle's martial wisdom into cybersecurity can mitigate potential risks through proactive defense and preparation. Just as nations allocate resources to their military to prevent conflicts and maintain security on a larger scale, individuals and corporations invest in cybersecurity to combat cyber threats and maintain digital peace.

The wise man hides his weapons.

Lao Tzu

The classic saying of Lao Tzu, "The wise man hides his weapons," sums together the qualities of caution, discernment, and the calculated hiding of important assets. This idea applies to many facets of life, such as cybersecurity, where protecting confidential information and assets is crucial.

In the context of cybersecurity, minimizing the visibility of vital assets aligns with the prudence of hiding one's weaponry. For instance, it makes sense for a business to limit how much of its intellectual property or sensitive information it discloses to the public. By implementing steps to restrict access to such assets, the organization improves its security posture and lowers the risk of potential cyber threats.

The concept of "security through obscurity" is one way to apply this principle. This approach uses information and system confidentiality as an additional line of defense, but it is not the only one. For example, hiding the source code of important software could make it harder for hackers to exploit security vulnerabilities.

Securing administrative access is a crucial security step analogous to concealing firearms. Limiting privileged access to authorized personnel and protecting sensitive account information are ways organizations reduce the risk of unauthorized breaches. Furthermore, modifying software signatures, such as changing OS designations from Windows to Linux or Cisco to Juniper, can conceal system types, potentially thwarting would-be attackers.

Lao Tzu's saying essentially emphasizes the value of exercising strategic prudence and protecting valuable assets. This wisdom aligns with cybersecurity best practices, which strengthen defenses against potential attackers by limiting exposure, implementing multiple layers of protection, and safeguarding important data. When individuals and organizations follow the prudent advice to hide their "weapons," they exercise caution and judgment in digital contexts, thereby enhancing overall security.

Carelessness is a great enemy.

Japanese Proverb

Beyond all eras and technological advancements, the Japanese proverb "Carelessness is a great enemy" resounds as eternal wisdom. It is a sobering reminder that our carelessness rather than outside influences often pose the most risks. This proverbial saying has special meaning in the context of cybersecurity, emphasizing how crucial it is to maintain constant watchfulness and diligence when protecting digital assets.

The dangers of negligence have increased in the digital age since large volumes of data are shared and stored online. Frequently, cyberattacks take advantage of small mistakes like weak passwords, unpatched software, or inadvertently clicking on phishing emails. These seemingly harmless mistakes can have serious repercussions, such as data breaches, harm to one's reputation, and large financial losses. As a result, the adage is a stinging reminder to use caution and heightened awareness when using contemporary technologies.

The wisdom in this proverb aligns with the concept of "least privilege." Organizations can lessen the potential harm caused by neglect, whether intentional or unintentional, by limiting individuals' access levels to only what is required for their responsibilities. Conducting routine audits and assessments of access credentials becomes essential to stop careless acts from unintentionally exposing vital systems and data.

Constant surveillance and documentation of network activities represent an additional essential cybersecurity tactic in keeping with the proverb's advice to avoid becoming careless. These procedures entail close observation of user behavior and network data to quickly identify and stop any unexpected or unauthorized activities. This painstaking attention to detail makes it easier to identify possible security vulnerabilities early on, which frequently result from seemingly harmless negligent actions.

The proverb also emphasizes the importance of continuous education and awareness campaigns for all staff members in a company. In cybersecurity systems, human mistakes are often the weakest link. Frequent training ensures that staff members are knowledgeable about current cyber threats, aware of the consequences of carelessness, and able to avoid common mistakes such as phishing scams.

In essence, the age-old Japanese saying "Carelessness is a great enemy" imparts a powerful lesson on the necessity of diligence and attention to detail in the cybersecurity landscape. Adopting principles like least privilege, continuous monitoring, and thorough employee training is essential at a time when carelessness with digital devices can have disastrous consequences. This timeless wisdom guides us toward a more cautious and secure approach to cyber protection as we navigate the complexities of the digital environment.

To spare the ravening leopard is an act of injustice to the sheep.

Persian Proverb

Despite its pastoral beginnings, the Persian saying, "To spare the ravening leopard is an act of injustice to the sheep," poignantly illustrates the value of justice and protection. It also makes a compelling analogy to the field of digital defense.

The "ravening leopard" is a metaphor used to describe the various hazards that can be found in cyberspace, such as malware, viruses, hackers, and other hostile entities. These digital lions are always on the lookout for openings in networks and systems to prey on. On the other hand, the "sheep" represent the priceless digital assets of a business, which include financial records, sensitive data, user personal information, and vital infrastructure systems.

Cybersecurity professionals and companies should not minimize or ignore the risks that could be posed by cyberattacks, just as a shepherd would be foolish to ignore the harm a leopard poses to his flock. The adage emphasizes the necessity of proactive defense, stressing the need to recognize and eliminate threats before they have a chance to cause harm.

The concept of "defense in depth" in cybersecurity aligns with this idea, promoting the use of multiple layers of security controls and defenses. By implementing a robust, multi-layered security framework, organizations can prevent a wide range of cyber risks. It's akin to making a leopard's habitat uninhabitable before it even approaches.

The proverb also emphasizes the ethical responsibility that cybersecurity entails. Safeguarding the interests and well-being of users, clients, employees, stakeholders, and citizens requires a commitment to protecting data and digital infrastructure. This goes beyond simple technological defense, as cybersecurity lapses can have far-reaching effects, jeopardizing personal safety, financial security, and integrity, along with legal repercussions.

The adage serves as a timely reminder of the critical importance of vigilance and preparedness in the contemporary digital environment as data breaches and cyberattacks become more complex and frequent. Cybersecurity thus becomes a strategic and moral imperative necessary for ensuring justice and safety. It calls for a proactive and resolute response to digital threats.

Ultimately, the timeless wisdom of the Persian adage significantly impacts cybersecurity, supporting a firm commitment to protecting the vulnerable and preserving digital integrity. Failure to address and mitigate digital risks results in ongoing injustice and insecurity in the digital realm. This jeopardizes the security of those entrusted to our care and emboldens the virtual "leopards."

The best armor is to keep out of range.

Italian Proverb

An ancient Italian adage that says, "The best armor is to keep out of range," offers important cybersecurity advice. Although brief, this suggestion develops into a proactive defensive approach that promotes avoidance as the primary means of resistance. It clarifies the idea of minimizing vulnerability by limiting exposure to possible hazards.

System hardening is a strategy that embodies the notion of remaining "out of range" when it comes to cyber protection. This procedure includes setting up networks, operating systems, and applications to be as secure as possible. Reducing user rights, blocking redundant ports, and disabling unnecessary services reduces attack vectors and protects vital resources from attackers.

Moreover, the implementation of network segmentation follows the proverb's guidance by dividing the digital terrain into discrete, smaller sections. By restricting possible damage and blocking attackers' lateral moves inside the network, this tactical division lessens the impact of breaches and keeps the bulk of the system "out of range."

The proverb also highlights the significance of proactive threat intelligence and vigilance. Keeping up with new threats and vulnerabilities helps firms foresee and mitigate hazards before they are taken advantage of. By using this proactive approach, valuable assets are moved out of the way of recognized risks.

The adage emphasizes the need for human awareness in cybersecurity, going beyond technological protections. Employees trained to spot phishing efforts, use strong passwords, and follow security guidelines strengthen the human firewall and reduce the possibility of human mistakes.

The Italian proverb, taken as a whole, sums up the core cybersecurity doctrine of putting an emphasis on preventative measures, minimizing attack surfaces, and reducing vulnerabilities. Taking a proactive approach to protection and prevention strengthens an organization's security posture in the dynamic realm of cyber threats by keeping vital resources safely "out of range" of prospective attackers.

What is of supreme importance in war is to attack the enemy's strategy.

Sun Tzu

The age-old counsel of Sun Tzu, "What is of supreme importance in war is to attack the enemy's strategy," attests to the necessity of comprehending, foreseeing, and outwitting the enemy's game plan to win. Despite being developed in the context of historical conflicts, this idea is extremely applicable to the state of cybersecurity today, particularly considering frameworks like MITRE ATT&CK.

The MITRE ATT&CK (Adversarial Tactics, Techniques, and Common Knowledge) framework is an expansive and evolving knowledge base that outlines the tactics, techniques, and procedures (TTPs) employed by adversaries in cyber campaigns. It is essentially an attempt to comprehend the "strategy" of cyber attackers, much to what Sun Tzu stressed. Defenders can better predict and resist hostile operations by knowing and recording these TTPs.

By incorporating Sun Tzu's ideas into the MITRE framework, the focus moves from reactive security measures to proactive ones. Comprehending the adversary's strategy enables defenders to anticipate the next attack's source, form, and potential consequences instead of just erecting walls and hoping they hold. It's the distinction between controlling the board and playing a reactive game.

Think about a well-known cyber-espionage organization with a history of attacking vital infrastructure across multiple nations. According to the MITRE ATT&CK framework, their known TTPs may entail spear-phishing attacks followed by lateral network moves to obtain elevated privileges. A defending business can tighten its email filters, inform staff members about the risks of phishing emails, keep an eye out for any strange lateral movements occurring within its network, and impose strict access controls by being aware of this tactic.

Organizations can also use technologies like honeypots to anticipate adversaries' activities, mislead them, waste their time and resources, and simultaneously learn more about their techniques. However, the core of Sun Tzu's wisdom transcends these details. It alludes to a foundational philosophy emphasizing the value of constant learning, adapting, and staying one step ahead in the field of cybersecurity. As adversarial strategies evolve with the digital landscape, it becomes crucial to continually analyze, anticipate, and counter the enemy's changing tactics, not just understand their current approach.

Combining Sun Tzu's age-old knowledge with contemporary cyber defense frameworks, such as MITRE ATT&CK, serves as a reminder that while tools and technologies evolve, strategic principles remain timeless. The ability to decipher and disrupt the enemy's strategy effectively determines success on the digital battlefield.

Reputation often spills less blood.

Samurai Maxim

The ancient Samurai proverb, "Reputation often spills less blood," has deep meaning and emphasizes how important a good reputation is for averting danger before it arises. The samurai, the elite soldiers of medieval Japan, knew that sometimes maintaining a strong reputation could prevent conflicts before they even started. The very fact that they were facing a well-known samurai would often deter would-be attackers from challenging them, saving both parties from the bloodshed that would otherwise ensue.

The modern digital era can benefit from this samurai wisdom, especially in the realm of cybersecurity. In this context, reputation can be built on a company's security procedures, proactive measures, and robust defenses. Just as a samurai's reputation might dissuade potential enemies, a business with a strong reputation for having skilled staff and effective cybersecurity protocols can deter hackers from attempting to compromise the organization.

Consider a large technology company known for making significant investments in cybersecurity, conducting frequent security audits, and swiftly addressing vulnerabilities. Given this reputation, cybercriminals may reconsider their efforts to breach its systems. In sharp contrast, a lesser-known business that hasn't developed a similar reputation may be seen as an easy target. Without the protection of a solid cybersecurity reputation, potential attackers may view this organization as easy pickings. Predators, whether in the wild or in cyberspace, will always look for easy prey. They rarely attack strong animals or entities due to the higher risk of harm.

The principle is the same in both scenarios—the digital world and the samurai battlefield: having a strong reputation can serve as a first line of defense. This reputation can be cultivated in cybersecurity through consistent training, regular updates to security protocols, prompt action in the face of attacks, and open and honest communication of security measures with relevant parties.

Though a good reputation can serve as a deterrent, it shouldn't breed complacency. The world of cybersecurity is constantly evolving, with new threats emerging daily. Even the most reputable organizations must continually maintain and strengthen their defenses. However, as the samurai proverb reminds us, in some cases, maintaining a good reputation can shield us from conflict, protect resources, and ensure peace.

Rely not on the likelihood of the enemy's not coming, but on our own readiness to receive him; not on the chance of his not attacking, but rather on the fact that we have made our position unassailable.

Sun Tzu

In the digital battlefield of cybersecurity, Sun Tzu's wise counsel to "rely not on the likelihood of the enemy's not coming, but on our own readiness to receive him; not on the chance of his not attacking, but rather on the fact that we have made our position unassailable" is as relevant as it is in conventional warfare. This idea emphasizes the need to plan and be proactive. It teaches us that the robustness of our defenses should always be our guarantee against any attack, not our want to avoid detection.

This knowledge translates into an always-prepared attitude in the cybersecurity space, where businesses and individuals operate on the presumption that a cyberattack is not just possible but inevitable. Because of this "assume breach" stance, organizations must remain vigilant and fortify their digital defenses against the continual danger of cyberattacks. By continuously looking for indications of compromise or hostile activity, intrusion detection and prevention systems (IDPS) embody Sun Tzu's advice to establish an impregnable stance against enemies.

Moreover, cybersecurity procedures like threat information collection and risk assessment mirror Sun Tzu's advice to "be aware of your surroundings." Organizations participate in a sort of digital reconnaissance by actively monitoring the cyber threat environment, identifying weaknesses within their systems, and strategically positioning themselves to confront new attacks through threat hunting.

Sun Tzu's advice fundamentally emphasizes maintaining constant watchfulness, making strategic plans, and anticipating dangers before they materialize. It advocates for a security posture that prioritizes ongoing observation, gathering threat information, actively seeking out threats, and implementing preventive measures. In addition to being aligned with the wisdom of being ready for the unexpected, this strategy ensures that an organization's digital domain is as impregnable as possible, demonstrating the enduring applicability of Sun Tzu's methods in the era of cyberwarfare.

Do not be tricked into thinking that there are no crocodiles just because the water is still.

Malaysian Proverb

The Malaysian proverb, "Do not be tricked into thinking that there are no crocodiles just because the water is still," is a potent metaphor for vigilance and caution, particularly pertinent in the context of cybersecurity. This proverb tells us not to get a false sense of security when things seem calm. It reminds us that risks are often hidden below the surface, waiting to be found.

This saying really hits home when it comes to safety. The digital world can often appear calm and safe, like still water. If systems are working well and there don't seem to be any problems or risks, it might create a false sense of security. But just like calm water can hide crocodiles, this calmness in digital systems can conceal weak spots, undetected breaches, and hidden cyber threats.

This proverb highlights the importance of being proactive about security rather than reactive. In cybersecurity, this means continuously monitoring systems and networks, even when there are no apparent signs of trouble. For example, advanced persistent threats (APTs) can infiltrate systems and remain dormant for months or even years, making them difficult to detect. To uncover these hidden threats, it is crucial to keep security measures up to date, conduct regular audits, and perform penetration tests.

The saying also emphasizes the importance of taking a comprehensive view of security. Focusing solely on strengthening perimeter defenses is not enough. Crocodiles can sneak up from deep underwater, and cyber threats can also arise from within your organization, either through insider threats or seemingly benign software vulnerabilities. It is essential to have a defense plan that addresses both internal and external threats.

Additionally, the proverb can be interpreted as a call for continuous education and awareness. In cybersecurity, keeping up with the latest threat landscapes, new attack methods, and technological trends is like watching still water for signs of movement. Other defenses include educating employees to recognize and report potential phishing attempts, promoting safe browsing habits, and fostering a culture that prioritizes cybersecurity.

In the end, the wise words of the Malaysian proverb teach us a timeless lesson: don't let appearances make you complacent. In life and in cybersecurity, the greatest threats are often the ones you cannot see immediately. Being constantly alert, taking a proactive approach to security, and cultivating a culture of awareness within an organization are all essential strategies to ensure that the still waters of our digital ecosystems do not conceal unseen dangers.

You must be deadly serious in training.

Gichin Funakoshi

Gichin Funakoshi's advice to take training seriously reverberates across the cybersecurity space, particularly in the demanding environments of Capture the Flag (CTF) cyber ranges. These platforms provide cyber warriors with a rich environment to hone their abilities against various digital foes, much like the demanding dojos of martial arts.

Think of the enthusiast who approaches the virtual arenas of HackTheBox or TryHackMe with the same intensity as a karateka walking into the dojo. They approach CTF tasks with an intensity akin to a martial artist's focused concentration, devoting hours to analyze weaknesses, plan intrusions, and carry out assaults with accuracy. Every task is combat, a trial of their skills, requiring not just technical proficiency but also a warrior's mindset of perseverance, skepticism, and creative problem-solving.

This sincere attempt at cyber-training embraces the ideas of Funakoshi. Cybersecurity enthusiasts develop their talents in the virtual dojos of CTF arenas, just as martial artists refine their trade via unrelenting practice, repetition, and reflection. They realize that proficiency in cybersecurity requires serious, committed practice, much as in martial arts, and cannot be attained with random attempts. Every CTF challenge is a step closer to excellence, providing a realistic danger simulation that hones their skills in thinking like an attacker and, in turn, a defense.

Through the adoption of Funakoshi's philosophy, participants in cybersecurity training go beyond simple engagement and embark on a path of ongoing development and adaptation. Just as martial arts training requires a "deadly serious" attitude, cyberwarfare carries significant risks. The knowledge gained in these cyber dojos extends beyond technical expertise; it instills participants with a mindset that enables them to navigate the constantly changing cybersecurity environment with agility and foresight.

Ultimately, Funakoshi's "deadly serious" approach to cybersecurity training equips students for both the broader fight against cyber dangers and the challenges encountered in CTF (Capture The Flag) competitions. This unwavering dedication to growth and learning strengthens digital frontiers and makes cyberspace safer. It reaffirms the timeless truth that significant achievement requires a great deal of commitment and discipline in the training process, whether in the physical or virtual worlds.

He is victorious who knows when and when not to fight.

Sun Tzu

The key to real success, according to Sun Tzu's profound military wisdom, is knowing when to fight in battle and when to avoid it strategically. It highlights the significance of intelligence and discernment in determining when to engage in combat and when to look for other options.

A successful warrior is not just one who can dominate their enemies in battle but also has a great understanding of the dynamics of the battlefield. They understand the importance of timing and that having a disagreement at the right time can result in a win-win situation.

Similarly, understanding when to back off is just as important. The wise warrior understands that some battles are not worth the price and that picking fights that are not necessary might have negative effects. They conserve resources and save energy for more important interactions by showing restraint and avoiding pointless conflicts.

This knowledge is applicable in many facets of life and transcends the battlefield. Successful businesspeople pick their battles carefully, deciding where to focus their time and energy for the greatest return on investment. Understanding when to be resolute and when to make concessions in interpersonal relationships promotes peace and understanding.

For instance, the cybersecurity professional may decide to use containment and observation rather than launching a quick counterattack when confronted with a modest cyber intrusion that offers little harm. They can develop a more effective defense plan by carefully observing the adversary's actions and gaining useful insights into the attacker's tactics and goals.

The smart cybersecurity expert may prioritize protecting crucial assets and data over direct confrontation in situations where a cyberattack poses an overwhelming threat to a system. To properly neutralize the danger, they might isolate the impacted components, implement backup and recovery protocols, and collaborate with law enforcement or other cybersecurity professionals.

This warrior wisdom encourages deliberate and methodical decision-making. By recognizing the value of timing and knowing when to fight and retreat, we can triumph in the challenges and undertakings that shape our lives and on the battlefield.

Focus on your one purpose.

Japanese Maxim

"Focus on your one purpose" is a Japanese proverb that sums up a simple but deep way of thinking. This knowledge comes from a society known for being very disciplined and paying close attention to details. It stresses the importance of focused effort and having a clear goal. In an era dominated by digital technology and cybersecurity challenges, the relevance of this maxim is particularly pronounced.

At its core, this Japanese wisdom encourages people to focus on their goals or tasks without distractions. In terms of cybersecurity, this means taking a focused approach to safeguarding digital assets. The digital world is vast and complex, with numerous potential vulnerabilities and risks. This adage would help a cybersecurity professional concentrate on the most critical aspects of security, ensuring that other issues do not distract them from their primary goals.

One concept in cybersecurity that aligns with this saying is "risk prioritization." Cybersecurity teams must constantly deal with various risks and vulnerabilities. By focusing on the most significant risks—the ones that would have the most substantial impact if exploited—security teams can better allocate their resources. This involves assessing threats based on their likelihood and potential severity, allowing for a targeted response to areas needing immediate attention.

The saying also suggests a deep commitment to one's chosen field or area of expertise. In the discipline of cybersecurity, this could mean becoming highly skilled in a particular domain, such as network security, threat analysis, or incident response. Given the broad scope of cybersecurity, professionals who excel in specific disciplines are invaluable.

The phrase "focus on your one purpose" can also guide organizations in protecting their data. A focused approach to security breaches can benefit companies, especially those with limited resources. Concentrating on the most critical assets or the most likely threat vectors can yield better security outcomes than attempting to cover all areas.

Maintaining this focused approach is crucial in the ever-evolving field of cybersecurity. While concentrating on a primary purpose or area, cybersecurity professionals must also remain adaptive and flexible, ready to shift their focus as new threats and technologies emerge.

Finally, the Japanese proverb "focus on your purpose" underscores the importance of directing our efforts and setting clear goals in a complex and dynamic field. This focused method can lead to stronger and more effective cybersecurity measures in resource allocation, expertise development, or defense planning. As with Japanese arts, the key lies in attention to detail, precision, and a steadfast dedication to the task at hand.

Tomorrow's battle is won during today's practice.

Samurai Maxim

"Tomorrow's battle is won during today's practice," as the Samurai stated, is a powerful saying that sums up how important it is to prepare and train, especially when facing difficulties and challenges. When it comes to cybersecurity, this concept is very important. To strengthen defenses against cyber threats that are always changing, you need proactive strategies, ongoing training, and hands-on simulations.

This Samurai wisdom is evident in many cybersecurity practices designed to enhance a company's safety. One great example is the use of "red team" and "blue team" exercises. During such exercises, the red team acts as the enemy, attempting to breach the organization's cyber defenses. In contrast, the blue team defends against cyber threats. These routines are not just drills but crucial training sessions that simulate real attacks. By conducting these simulations, organizations not only test their response plans but also identify and address security vulnerabilities, making them better prepared for actual cyberattacks.

The maxim also highlights the importance of proper instruction for end users and IT staff. Because cyber threats often exploit human nature, educating employees about potential risks and how to avoid them is essential. When personnel receive regular cyber training, they learn to recognize signs of phishing, suspicious activities, and potential security weaknesses. Overall, this proactive approach to education significantly enhances a company's preparedness to deal with cyber threats.

Additionally, the maxim underscores the importance of testing employees' responses and readiness for phishing attacks through mock campaigns. Companies can evaluate the effectiveness of their training programs and identify areas needing improvement by regularly subjecting employees to simulated phishing attacks. This strategy aligns with the Samurai philosophy of honing one's skills today to achieve victory in future battles.

There is a clear connection between hacking and the Samurai proverb. The principle guides organizations in preparing for cyber threats by emphasizing the value of rigorous practice, continuous education, and preventive measures. This level of readiness is achieved through various methods, including red team/blue team exercises, comprehensive cybersecurity training, and mock phishing campaigns. In a constantly evolving digital world, this approach keeps an organization's defenses robust and ready, adhering to the Samurai way of meticulously preparing for future challenges.

The bird that offers itself to the net is fair game to the fowler.

Japanese Proverb

The Japanese proverb beautifully captures the essence of being fragile and careful. It is a strong warning of how dangerous it is to be careless with your exposure and how important it is to be alert. This proverb compares someone's careless exposure to a bird going into a net without knowing it. It means that when we put ourselves in dangerous situations without being careful, we leave ourselves open to being taken advantage of.

Consider the all-too-common situation in the digital world where an employee receives an email that appears harmless but requests private information, such as login details. If the employee complies without verifying the request's authenticity, they unwittingly expose themselves and their company to online threats. In this scenario, the cyberattacker is like the fowler, cleverly setting traps to exploit someone's trust, allowing them to access private data or systems without permission.

This situation underscores the critical importance of user awareness and vigilance regarding cybersecurity risks. It is vital for individuals to exercise caution and discernment when communicating online. Avoiding falling prey to cyberattackers' tactics requires actions such as carefully scrutinizing emails for signs of phishing and being wary of social engineering.

The proverb advises us to exercise caution in our actions and decision-making. It warns against carelessly exposing vulnerabilities or placing undue trust in others without verifying their trustworthiness. Instead, it encourages us to remain alert and watchful, helping us protect ourselves from harm.

This ancient wisdom highlights the importance of being careful in our interactions, especially in a digital world where not everyone has good intentions. It emphasizes the need for vigilance and self-protection in an environment where threats can emerge from any direction.

Ultimately, this warrior wisdom provides a timeless lesson on the importance of recognizing potential threats and taking measures to protect ourselves from exploitation. By minimizing unnecessary risks, we can maintain security and build resilience in the face of various challenges.

This prudent and cautious approach can guide us through the complex and often dangerous landscape of cybersecurity.

Freedom is the only worthy goal in life. It is won by disregarding things that lie beyond our control.

Epictetus

The stoic philosopher Epictetus famously declared, "The only worthwhile objective in life is freedom." It is achieved by ignoring factors outside of our control." In the field of cybersecurity, there is a specific reality to this deep remark. In this sense, freedom can be understood as the condition of being safe and free from cyberthreats; this is a goal that is attained by concentrating on what can be successfully controlled and managed inside an organization's cybersecurity framework rather than worrying about the abundance of uncontrollable external threats.

One of the most important things a business can manage is the deployment of robust passphrases and other security measures. The first line of defense for protecting digital assets is a strong password. It is a straightforward control strategy that significantly lowers the likelihood of unauthorized access. Organizations take proactive measures to strengthen their systems against infiltration by creating complex, unique passphrases and changing them often.

Another essential component of an organization's management is the ongoing training of staff members on cyber threats. Epictetus's philosophy places a strong emphasis on knowledge and readiness. By educating employees about the most recent cyber threats and their manifestations, as well as recommended security procedures, companies enable their workforce to participate actively in their defense. This continuous training makes employees aware of possible risks and how to respond to them, much like preparing soldiers for combat.

Moreover, the idea of routine testing and assessment of cybersecurity measures is consistent with the philosophy of focusing on what is within our control. Companies can manage their security effectively through monthly email phishing campaigns. By regularly simulating phishing attempts, they assess their employees' alertness and pinpoint areas where additional training may be needed. These campaigns serve as a training tool and an evaluation of how well previous instruction was received.

Another way to apply Epictetus's advice is by holding frequent red-blue team drills. During these drills, the blue team (defenders) strives to stop the red team (attackers) from breaching the organization's defenses using known adversarial tactics, techniques, and procedures (TTP). This continuous cycle of attack and defense is a strategic move to stay ahead of potential adversaries. It exemplifies the idea of focusing on the cybersecurity team's preparedness and responsiveness—what is within our control. These drills reveal areas needing improvement and provide invaluable insights into the current effectiveness of security mechanisms.

In conclusion, cybersecurity greatly benefits from Epictetus's idea of pursuing freedom by concentrating on what is within your control. Organizations take control of their cybersecurity by using strong passphrases, regularly training staff, running phishing simulations, and conducting red team/blue team drills. They create an environment where protection against cyberattacks is a realistic objective achieved through vigilance, preparedness, and proactive defensive techniques. As Epictetus put it, cybersecurity is just the desire for freedom, which we achieve by mastering the things we can manage

Though we are powerful and strong, and we know how to fight, we do not wish to fight.

Cherokee Saying

The Cherokee proverb, "Even though we are strong and powerful and know how to fight, we do not wish to fight," teaches important lessons about the morality of strength and the value of harmony over strife. This idea, which has its roots in a society that cherishes harmony and balance, provides a useful foundation for comprehending cybersecurity. It argues that having the capacity to engage in digital battles does not necessitate their use; instead, it promotes the careful, moral application of skills and expertise in the digital sphere.

This perspective highlights the difference between being in a position of power and deciding when and how to wield it. Like the warriors mentioned in the Cherokee proverb, cybersecurity experts can technically initiate offensive cyber operations. However, it is morally imperative to use these powers defensively—to safeguard and defend rather than to attack. This strategy aligns with the overarching objectives of cybersecurity, which include data security, maintaining system integrity, and ensuring the welfare of online communities and organizations.

The proverb also emphasizes the importance of proactive protection in cybersecurity. By focusing on strengthening cyber defenses, conducting comprehensive vulnerability assessments, and training users on cybersecurity best practices, potential attackers may be deterred, reducing the need for physical confrontations. Cybersecurity initiatives that prioritize defense help create a stable and secure digital environment, lessening the likelihood of cyber warfare.

Furthermore, Cherokee wisdom encourages a cautious response to cybersecurity events. It suggests that instead of reacting hastily, one should carefully evaluate the circumstances, understand the nature of the attack, mitigate its effects, and strengthen defenses to prevent recurrence. This approach ensures that responses are not only efficient but also contribute to the stability and long-term security of the digital ecosystem.

The proverb serves as a helpful reminder of the accountability that comes with authority, especially in cybersecurity. Experts in this field have substantial control over the security and safety of digital environments. They are responsible for using this authority wisely, prioritizing moral principles and the greater good over hostile or vengeful acts.

Essentially, the cybersecurity industry can greatly benefit from the wisdom provided by this Cherokee proverb. It promotes standing in a position of power and readiness, along with a commitment to moral behavior and the pursuit of peace. By adopting this prudent approach, cybersecurity experts can ensure their abilities are used appropriately, contributing to a digital environment where authority is exercised carefully to preserve peace and protect the collective digital welfare.

By keeping your weapons in order, your enemy will be subjugated.

Nagarjuna

Strategic forethought and efficient planning are encapsulated in Nagarjuna's sage warrior knowledge. It emphasizes the importance of staying disciplined and prepared, especially regarding one's tools or weapons, to defeat enemies. This idea, rooted in military strategy, is incredibly relevant to the cybersecurity industry.

The comparison to maintaining order in one's arsenal highlights the significance of preemptive preparation, following procedures, and maintaining a state of readiness for any eventuality. Just as a well-armed and well-prepared warrior has a major advantage in battle, having a clear strategy and being prepared for any situation provides a tactical advantage in overcoming obstacles and opponents.

This knowledge promotes a proactive strategy, suggesting that possessing the appropriate resources—including knowledge, abilities, and tools—is essential for overcoming a variety of challenges. By keeping everything in order and being ready, people can react quickly and decisively, reducing risks and maximizing efficiency.

This idea transcends its martial setting and can be applied to various aspects of life, such as career pursuits, personal objectives, and unforeseen obstacles. It emphasizes the importance of being well-prepared for diverse situations, whether pursuing personal goals, thriving in the workplace, or overcoming unexpected challenges.

This kind of thinking is applicable to effectively managing digital defenses in the context of cybersecurity. A cybersecurity expert is better able to repel online attacks if they maintain their digital "weapons"—firewalls, access restrictions, software updates, and patches—in excellent working condition. For instance, an organization can better manage potential cyber risks if it consistently updates and patches its software systems, imposes stringent access limits, and maintains strong firewalls.

Cybersecurity experts can keep their defenses well-organized and functional by closely monitoring network activity and staying updated on the latest threats and attack strategies. This proactive approach enables them to quickly identify breaches, take appropriate action to mitigate their effects, and hinder the activities of cybercriminals.

Furthermore, being ready for cybersecurity involves more than just technological measures. It also entails conducting frequent training sessions and teaching staff members about cybersecurity best practices. By instilling a security-conscious mindset in employees, cybersecurity experts provide an extra line of protection against human-centric cyberthreats like social engineering.

Essentially, we can develop a mindset of readiness and preparedness by following Nagarjuna's guidance. We can overcome barriers and reach our goals by organizing our resources, improving our abilities, and being ready for any difficulties. Maintaining the hierarchy of our "weapons," whether actual or symbolic, enables us to effectively overcome obstacles and accomplish our goals in various fields, including the crucial one of cybersecurity.

The path of the warrior is lifelong, and mastery is often simply staying on the path.

Richard Strozzi Heckler

The insightful quote by Richard Strozzi Heckler, "The path of the warrior is lifelong, and mastery is often simply staying on the path," speaks a great deal about the experiences that cybersecurity professionals have. This knowledge captures the spirit of an unrelenting quest for mastery, emphasizing the value of tenacity, never-ending education, and flexibility—essential qualities in the ever-changing field of cybersecurity.

Professionals in cybersecurity face a never-ending stream of challenges and constant changes in their field. Cyber threats form a dynamic and complex ecosystem where new vulnerabilities regularly appear and attacker techniques continually evolve. Therefore, cybersecurity professionals must be vigilant and dedicated to keeping up with the latest developments in their field.

In cybersecurity, staying on the warrior's path involves continually seeking opportunities to advance one's knowledge and skills. This endeavor includes participating in various educational activities such as self-directed study, formal training and certifications, capture-the-flag competitions, and practical experience. It also entails keeping up with the latest developments in cybersecurity, including trends, threats, and technologies, to adjust plans and approaches accordingly.

Heckler's observation emphasizes the value of resilience in the face of difficulty. Cybersecurity professionals must be prepared to encounter obstacles and failures and turn them into learning opportunities. This resilience includes mental fortitude, the ability to remain calm under duress, and technical proficiency.

Adopting Heckler's concept also involves developing an attitude of constant improvement. This means not just defending against current threats but also anticipating future challenges. It entails taking a proactive stance, from creating and testing incident response strategies to regularly auditing systems. Through innovation and information exchange, cybersecurity professionals improve not just their immediate security posture but also the sector as a whole.

Finally, the insights of Richard Strozzi Heckler provide a potent perspective for those working in cybersecurity. In this sector, mastery is a journey requiring constant commitment, learning, and flexibility rather than an endpoint. Cybersecurity experts who choose the warrior path dedicate themselves to a never-ending quest for excellence, always honing their skills to defend against the ever-changing dangers in the digital realm. This path creates individuals who are not just adept at their trade but also resilient, adaptive, and perpetually vigilant. It is as much about personal development as it is about professional proficiency.

Think, feel, and act like a warrior. Set yourself apart from the rest of society by your personal excellence.

Forrest E. Morgan

The advice given by Forrest E. Morgan to "think, feel, and act like a warrior" is a strong exhortation to live a life that embodies warriorship in all aspects and to set oneself apart by personal excellence. This guidance forces us to embrace excellence from all angles, incorporating it into our feelings, ideas, and behaviors to elevate our lives above the norm.

Thinking like a warrior means putting on a resilient, clear, and strategically foresighted mindset. It entails creating an internal environment in which obstacles are seen as chances for development and failures are seen as possibilities for learning. A warrior's mindset is based on vision and purpose, which allows for quick decision-making and perceptive situational analysis, all with the ultimate objective of conquering challenges and coming out stronger.

Being emotionally in control and cultivating a strong sense of inner stability and power are necessary for feeling like a warrior. It has to do with cultivating an emotional intelligence that permits recognition of feelings without letting them control behavior. This self-control and awareness guarantee that a warrior stays cool under pressure, prepared to act with precision rather than haste, whether in a physical or metaphorical conflict.

Being a warrior takes you beyond the lines of combat. It is a dedication to leading a life consistent with the greatest ideals of honor, integrity, and ongoing personal development. This route entails a constant pursuit of intellectual advancement, moral purity, or physical prowess as measures of personal development. A code of excellence that requires not just skill in their profession but also a noble nature and an unrelenting dedication to doing what is right governs the warrior's conduct.

Morgan's way of thinking encourages us to live out the warrior ethos every day, impacting not just our own journeys but also the lives of people around us. By exhibiting brilliance, self-control, and fortitude, we encourage people to raise their bar and pursue greatness in their own lives.

In the end, following Forrest E. Morgan's description of the warrior's path is making the commitment to a life distinguished by continuous development, resiliency, and a deep commitment to moral and personal greatness. This dedication not only makes us stand out but also enhances the contributions we make to society, enabling us to be agents of good change and pillars of strength and morality in a world that is often turbulent.

The wise hawk conceals his talons.

Japanese Proverb

The Japanese adage "The wise hawk conceals his talons" powerfully illustrates the need for exercising control, strategic judgment, and respecting the hidden might that lies in reserve. It emphasizes that real strength and wisdom come from using one's powers wisely and deliberately when the time is right rather than from displaying one's might in an obvious way.

This idea has significant applications in the field of cybersecurity, where information disclosure or concealment can profoundly impact security outcomes. Like the astute hawk, cybersecurity experts recognize the importance of keeping their "talons"—their abilities, strategies, and breadth of knowledge—hidden from potential adversaries. By doing so, they maintain leverage and an element of surprise, which can be crucial in preventing cyber threats and attacks.

The adage emphasizes the importance of holding off on disclosing security tactics or vulnerabilities in cybersecurity. For example, carelessly disseminating knowledge about a discovered security vulnerability within a company can lead to its exploitation. Instead, a measured approach is preferred, which entails evaluating the vulnerability, understanding its implications, and discreetly developing a remediation strategy before the public discovers the flaw, if at all possible.

Furthermore, this mindset is applicable to the broader cybersecurity defensive strategy. Many advanced cybersecurity systems use obfuscation and concealment techniques, such as honeypots, to deceive and trap intruders. These strategies validate the wisdom of the adage by concealing the actual strengths and weaknesses of the system, thereby enhancing network security.

The wisdom of keeping one's claws hidden also applies to personal and professional development in the cybersecurity industry. Experts often work on sensitive projects or develop innovative solutions that, if revealed too soon, may lose their advantageous effects or be co-opted by competitors. Therefore, it is sensible to be strategically quiet and to share one's accomplishments and ideas when the timing and context are appropriate.

"The wise hawk conceals his talons" essentially captures a timeless strategy that transcends cultures and eras and finds relevance in the complex battlefield of cybersecurity. It emphasizes wisdom lies in knowing when to act and when to hold back to ensure one's actions are decisive, effective, and impactful. This traditional wisdom promotes a measured response to challenges and a deliberate use of one's skills to maximize stability, achievement, and goal fulfillment.

In order to progress in life, one has to improve every day in an endless process.

The Hagakure

The Hagakure stresses the value of ongoing development and self-improvement because of its deep understanding of the warrior's mentality. This knowledge, which is fundamental to warrior culture, emphasizes that development is a lifelong process and is necessary for success in all spheres of endeavor.

This school of thought warns against the dangers of stagnation and complacency, which obstruct the pursuit of greatness and self-improvement. Instead, it promotes an unrelenting quest for knowledge, introspection, and improvement. Just as a proficient fighter refines their skills through constant practice and devotion, we are inspired to commit to bettering ourselves in various areas of life, such as moral rectitude, emotional intelligence, mental clarity, and physical fitness.

The applicability of The Hagakure's counsel is especially noteworthy for a cybersecurity expert. Maintaining a competitive edge in an industry marked by rapid changes, emerging risks, and developing technology requires steadfast dedication to continuous improvement and education.

A cybersecurity specialist subscribing to this school of thought understands the importance of staying up to date on the most recent advancements in the industry. They might set aside time each day to join online forums, participate in webinars, interact with industry publications, and stay informed about the latest developments in cybersecurity. Their dedication to education enhances their awareness of new risks and provides them with the most up-to-date security techniques.

Like a warrior, a cybersecurity professional must hone their technical skills through hands-on training in addition to their academic understanding. This might include tackling real-world security challenges, participating in simulated exercises, and receiving practical training. These activities refine their skills, improve their ability to recognize and neutralize threats and ensure they remain effective in their responsibilities.

Furthermore, The Hagakure's mission encompasses the cultivation of soft skills essential for a cybersecurity practitioner. These include leadership, problem-solving, and communication skills necessary to succeed in their roles and work well in teams.

By adopting a continuous improvement mindset, a cybersecurity professional can facilitate a learning culture within their organization. This strategy fosters information exchange and strengthens a robust cybersecurity posture. As they become role models, they inspire others to embrace a growth-oriented mentality and promote creativity and flexibility in response to constantly evolving cyber threats.

The Hagakure encourages us to see obstacles as opportunities for development and acknowledges that the pursuit of greatness is a lifelong effort. Every day offers a fresh opportunity to strengthen our weaknesses, learn from our mistakes, and build on our strengths.

By embracing this warrior wisdom, we take charge of our growth and continuously push the boundaries to achieve more ambitious goals. We live meaningful lives and leave a legacy of development and greatness when we consistently strive for progress.

Take away the cause, and the effect ceases.

Miguel de Cervantes

In his perceptive knowledge, Miguel de Cervantes emphasizes the essential idea that issues should be addressed at their core to lessen their impact. He says, "Take away the cause, and the effect ceases," giving clear instructions on how to address problems at their root rather than just masking their symptoms.

This insight emphasizes the need to approach problem-solving proactively. It implies that solving an issue by focusing solely on its surface level may provide short-term relief but not a long-term fix. Finding and addressing the problem's root cause will lead to a true resolution.

This type of thinking is essential to a warrior's strategy. Warriors understand the value of addressing the root causes of conflicts rather than merely responding to their symptoms, much like strategic thinkers do. This enhanced understanding leads to more robust and efficient solutions.

Utilizing cybersecurity as an example provides a pertinent and practical application of this concept. Imagine a situation where an organization experiences recurrent data breaches due to staff members' weak passwords. Merely reacting to each security issue as it arises might provide temporary solutions. However, tackling the underlying issue head-on with multi-factor authentication, staff training, and strong password policies is a more effective approach. By eliminating the core problem of weak password security, the company can prevent future breaches and their potentially disastrous outcomes.

This cybersecurity case study highlights the importance of addressing fundamental problems. Cybersecurity experts know that the only way to ensure the long-term security of digital systems is to locate and fix vulnerabilities at their roots. As the saying goes, eliminating the cause successfully prevents the effect.

In the end, Cervantes' insight underscores the significance of understanding the underlying causes of situations and acting proactively to resolve them. In the world of military strategy or cybersecurity, the ability to focus on root causes enables individuals to anticipate and prevent unfavorable consequences, resulting in long-lasting effects and solutions. This method embodies a concept of comprehensive and efficient problem-solving, as it not only fixes current problems but also safeguards against future threats.

It is no honor for an eagle to vanquish a dove.

Italian Proverb

In the context of leadership and mentoring, especially in the field of cybersecurity, the Italian proverb "It is no honor for an eagle to vanquish a dove" eloquently captures the essence of true dignity and nobility. This wisdom reminds us that elevating and leading those who are less powerful is a better way to show genuine respect instead of subduing them.

This adage contrasts the dove, a representation of peace and fragility, with the eagle, a symbol of strength and power. The message is clear: showing dominance over those who are weaker does not truly honor a person with strength and skill. True honor, on the other hand, comes from using one's skills to uplift and serve.

This viewpoint is particularly pertinent to cybersecurity, a field with a dynamic and complicated environment. Like the eagle, an experienced cybersecurity specialist is in a position of strength and wisdom. The adage supports a mentoring role rather than exploiting this position to denigrate or overshadow less seasoned team members.

In this context, the cybersecurity specialist might act as a mentor, imparting expertise and offering advice to team members who are less experienced. This might include educating them on the most recent attacks and protection techniques, assisting them in overcoming challenging security situations or providing guidance on how to advance in a cybersecurity career. The goal is to empower these individuals and assist them in developing and enhancing their abilities.

This kind of strategy not only makes the team stronger but also promotes a happy, cooperative workplace. The specialist contributes to the development of a more competent and resilient cybersecurity team by fostering talent and growth. The proverb's advice to use one's power for the improvement and elevation of others rather than for dominance is consistent with the mentoring role.

Cybersecurity professionals may leave a legacy of respect and dignity by emulating this insight. They have the power to transform their workplace into a place where people respect each other's dignity, exchange information, and develop together. By doing this, they support the moral and admirable practice of mentoring in the realm of cybersecurity, in addition to improving the skills of their team.

Noblemen discipline themselves to be dignified at all times... Sharpen your mind and show your dignity.

Matsura Seizen

In his deep exposition of martial wisdom, Matsura Seizen emphasizes the qualities of mental acuity, disciplined behavior, and noblesse oblige. He explains how maintaining self-control is essential to upholding one's dignity and intellectual growth.

This knowledge is based on the behavior of noblemen, who are models of composure and self-control under all conditions. No matter what obstacles or feelings they encounter, they are known for their capacity to maintain composure and dignity. Their unwavering composure under duress is evidence of their disciplined way of living.

The advice to "sharpen your mind" emphasizes how crucial mental clarity and intellectual advancement are. A noble-minded person is dedicated to learning new things and developing a deeper understanding of the world, much like a wise fighter. In addition to learning new things, the quest for wisdom involves honing one's critical thinking and reasoning skills. By reading this book, you are making the wise choice to sharpen your warrior mindset.

By virtue of his embrace of self-control and keen intellect, the noble warrior is well-suited to dealing with life's difficulties. They approach issues with mental clarity, discernment, and reason, which empowers them to make wise choices even in difficult and emotionally charged circumstances.

Furthermore, this martial knowledge combines noble behavior with the idea of honor. The noble warrior cultivates respect and integrity in their deeds and relationships by maintaining a dignified manner and honing the mind. This combination of intelligence and dignity produces an attitude that inspires confidence and commands respect.

Accepting the lessons of Matsura Seizen inspires us to live like honorable warriors. By exercising self-control, seeking intellectual advancement, and behaving honorably, we can overcome obstacles gracefully and positively impact those around us. This path of nobility and discipline sets an example for excellence and moral behavior while promoting personal growth and enriching our communities.

To be prepared for war is one of the most effective means of preserving peace.

George Washington

The proverbial "to be prepared for war is one of the most effective means of preserving peace," attributed to George Washington, sums up the concept of strategic deterrence in a variety of contexts, including the dynamic field of cybersecurity. This way of thinking emphasizes the need to be prepared and build strong defenses, which are essential to guarantee security and avoid confrontation.

This idea extends beyond the cybersecurity domain into the creation of a strong security posture that deters possible attackers. A well-defended network can stop cyber threats from materializing, just as a ready military can thwart aggression and uphold peace. It's all about establishing a readiness level that can fend off assaults and give prospective adversaries the impression that trying to breach defenses would be pointless and unsafe.

This readiness is shown by the use of cutting-edge security measures like strict access restrictions, encryption, and extensive threat detection systems. Regular security audits, penetration tests, and developing a security-aware culture among all personnel are comparable to military drills that keep soldiers sharp and prepared for any eventuality.

This proactive approach to cybersecurity raises the cost of an attack for hackers, acting as a deterrent. Attackers are more likely to go for simpler targets when they believe infiltrating a system would entail significant effort and a high risk of failure and discovery. Thus, by making an assault less appealing, the preparedness and strength of cybersecurity defenses directly contribute to the preservation of digital peace.

Furthermore, to strengthen collective security, this concept emphasizes the importance of organizations and countries working together and sharing information. Cybersecurity alliances may further maintain peace in the digital realm by offering shared warnings of new dangers, collaborating to develop defensive systems, and coordinating responses to threats, just as partnerships and alliances can boost military deterrence.

Washington's phrase essentially acts as a cornerstone for cybersecurity policies all over the globe. It serves as a reminder that our level of readiness and defense is a major factor in ensuring the safety and tranquility of our digital lives. Organizations that prioritize cybersecurity preparedness and invest in it safeguard themselves and advance the larger objective of fostering a more tranquil and safer online environment for everyone. This military readiness-inspired strategic approach to cybersecurity highlights the wisdom of Washington's enduring significance in directing our efforts to protect the digital frontier.

To subdue an enemy without fighting is the greatest of skills.

Sun Tzu

The centuries-old maxim of Sun Tzu, "To subdue an enemy without fighting is the greatest of skills," emphasizes the superiority of intelligence over force and calls for the adoption of tactics that eliminate threats without resorting to direct conflict. Despite having its roots in the ancient art of war, this idea is highly applicable to the field of cybersecurity today, as conflicts are now fought virtually rather than on actual battlefields.

Imagine a situation where skilled cybercriminals pose a constant threat to cybersecurity personnel. By adopting a more strategic, non-confrontational stance, these experts can reflect Sun Tzu's ideas instead of launching a retaliatory cyber assault that could exacerbate tensions or spark further attacks. This approach might include implementing sophisticated threat detection systems that detect and neutralize hostile activity covertly or using deception technologies like honeypots to trick attackers into disclosing their strategies without endangering the network itself.

Using knowledge and foresight to outmaneuver enemies and secure digital assets without the aftermath of a direct digital battle illustrates the concept of winning without fighting. The focus is on understanding the weaknesses and goals of the opposition and then developing defenses that work against them, all the while preventing the opponent from realizing they have been defeated until it is too late.

Beyond cybersecurity, this way of thinking promotes the use of strategic thinking in negotiation, dispute resolution, and even everyday interpersonal interactions. It suggests that objectives can be achieved and issues resolved more effectively and sustainably through understanding, diplomacy, and strategic planning rather than confrontation or aggression.

Sun Tzu's wisdom highlights the significance of strategic dominance, achieved through cunning, planning, and the ability to foresee and eliminate obstacles without engaging in open combat. It advocates for a mindset prioritizing stability and peace, attainable through strategy and intelligence rather than force.

Essentially, the capacity to defeat an opponent without engaging in combat indicates a mastery of strategy, demonstrating not just a superior understanding of conflict but also a strong commitment to maintaining peace. This idea provides a path to goals with the least resistance, whether applied in cybersecurity or more general life issues. It fosters an environment where success is achieved through insight and planning rather than force.

To see Is to be deceived, to feel is to know.

Corey M. Hubbert

We may learn a lot about life lessons from the traditional practices and teachings of martial arts. "To see is to be deceived, to feel is to know" is a lesson I like to share with my Jiu-Jitsu students. I believe that it relates to both the dojo and everyday life. This proverb teaches us that initial impressions aren't always true and illustrates how intuitive experiences and sentiments help us comprehend things more fully.

The adage is particularly true when it comes to Jiu-Jitsu, a martial art recognized for its techniques of off-balancing an opponent and using leverage. Practitioners often engage in close-quarters combat, relying more on their senses than visual cues to anticipate their adversaries' next move. Jiu-Jitsu practitioners may sense their opponent's weight shift, the tightening of muscles, a shift in balance, and sometimes even anticipate their opponent's techniques, countering them with intuition. The eyes may be tricked when this occurs. Even though an adversary may attempt to deceive you or conceal their intentions, the subtle physical cues they leave behind might reveal more about their future plans.

The saying extends this idea beyond the world of martial arts and applies it to all of life. In a time filled with a lot of information and visual stimulation, like constant social media feeds and videos, our eyes can often be overwhelmed. The world is made up of carefully crafted scams, filtered images, and well-rehearsed acts. Here, the word "seeing" can be a source of confusion, mistakes, and even deception. If we rely solely on visual cues, we might make errors, like misjudging a person's character based on their appearance, making decisions based on biased data, or clicking on a link from a well-crafted, deceptive phishing email.

Feeling, on the other hand, taps into a more basic, intuitive knowledge of the world. Emotions, gut reactions, and physical feelings can provide information your conscious, logical mind can't always see. When we say we "feel" a certain way about a choice, a person, or a situation, we mean that we have a gut feeling about it that isn't always backed up by facts but is still true. This gut feeling is often closer to the truth than what we see on the surface.

When you compare this conventional wisdom to modern problems like fake news or digital deception, the lesson is clear: a warrior needs to develop and trust the intuitive sense of right and wrong. In a world where images can be faked by AI and visual representations can be skewed, the most reliable method to find our way is through deeper, intuitive knowledge that comes from critical thinking, meditation, and personal experience.

Ultimately, my teachings serve as a potent reminder that relying solely on sight is insufficient and that strong intuitive knowledge might be more trustworthy. Whether we're looking to master a martial art or figure out how to navigate life, feeling our way through difficulties is frequently the most authentic and reliable approach to discovering knowledge and truth.

Make yourself a sheep, and the wolf is ready.

Russian Proverb

"Make yourself a sheep, and the wolf is ready" is a Russian adage that captures a timeless idea of vulnerability and tactic. It's a sobering reminder that showing signs of weakness—whether on purpose or accidentally—can draw enemies fast. This knowledge emphasizes the strategic use of vulnerabilities in the context of cybersecurity to draw attention to and comprehend possible threats, thus converting an apparent deficit into a tactical advantage.

The usage of honeypots in cybersecurity processes provides a striking example of this idea. Systems known as "honeypots" are made to look and feel like genuine network assets, making them attractive to hackers. Their actual objective is to track and examine the tactics, techniques, and procedures (TTPs) of the attackers. Organizations may attract 'wolves' and gain valuable knowledge on prospective threats without endangering the network itself by creating the appearance of weakness and modeling themselves like the 'sheep.'

A greater understanding of the nature of cyber threats and the psychology of attackers is reflected in the deliberate deployment of honeypots. It acknowledges that attackers often hunt for the easiest targets out of opportunism. Organizations may lower the risk to critical infrastructure by generating controlled vulnerabilities that allow them to identify and evaluate assaults while deflecting attention from real assets.

This adage also emphasizes the need to strategically manage one's weaknesses, whether fabricated or genuine. In the grand scheme of things, it implies that, when executed with planning and forethought, displaying weakness can sometimes be a very effective tactic. This chess-like aspect of cybersecurity defense requires a deep awareness of both one's own and the adversary's capabilities and limitations.

The use of this idea goes beyond the technological components of cybersecurity. It entails fostering an environment where any risks are not only acknowledged and dealt with but also anticipated and prepared for. It pushes companies to adopt an adversarial mindset, anticipating potential attack vectors and making appropriate preparations.

The Russian proverb essentially illuminates a highly developed method of strategic defense. It demonstrates that vulnerability may be used as a tool rather than only being feared as a weakness—both in cybersecurity and in life. Organizations may stay ahead of possible threats by strategically managing and sometimes even exposing vulnerabilities. This can help them turn the tables on attackers and improve their security posture in the constantly changing digital ecosystem.

A man who has attained mastery of an art reveals it in his every action.

Samurai Maxim

The adage among Samurai, "A man who has attained mastery of an art reveals it in his every action," conveys a great deal about the nature of actual skill and how it shows itself in every aspect of a person's behavior. It teaches us that mastery is more than simply ability; it's also the embodiment of wisdom, knowledge, and experience that penetrates all of the master's actions.

Within the domain of cybersecurity, this idea is demonstrated by experts whose every decision, evaluation, and reaction shows a profound comprehension and mastery of their subject. These professionals see cybersecurity as a way of life where their in-depth knowledge and refined instincts serve as their guides. They can identify risks others may miss, develop tasteful yet practical solutions, and confidently and strategically navigate the treacherous world of digital security. Their approach to cybersecurity problems shows not just technical skill but also a thorough grasp that informs each strategy, decision, and execution.

This adage emphasizes the path needed to reach this level of proficiency as well. It's a road characterized by never-ending study, consistent practice, and the unwavering quest for perfection. In this view, mastery is a lifelong endeavor—a continuous process of honing one's abilities, broadening one's knowledge, and skillfully and perceptively adapting to new challenges.

Furthermore, this maxim's underlying idea goes beyond the confines of any one profession to reflect the universal reality that genuine mastery is always shown by the practitioner's actions. People who have attained a high degree of expertise in their field—whether it be the humanities, sciences, arts, or technology—display this through their work, relationships with others, and approach to problem-solving.

In the end, this Samurai wisdom promotes a comprehensive approach to mastery by serving as a reminder that genuine expertise is not limited to technical proficiency but manifests in our attitudes, ethics, and interactions with the outside world. It is a call to action for cybersecurity professionals to protect digital assets with not just expertise and knowledge but also morality, accountability, and a dedication to the greater good. By striving to live up to our competence in all we do, we improve our own practice and help elevate the standards and effectiveness of our respective disciplines.

The important thing is to be always moving forward, little by little.

Masutatsu Oyama

The words of wisdom from Masutatsu Oyama, "The important thing is to be always moving forward, little by little," have a significant impact on the cybersecurity industry and beyond. They emphasize the value of incremental growth. It emphasizes the idea that gradual, steady progress eventually results in major accomplishments, stressing the need for tenacity and ongoing development in learning difficult subjects.

This is an essential technique in cybersecurity. The dynamic and intricate nature of digital threats necessitates constant adaptation on the part of specialists. In this field, significant advances in knowledge or capacity are uncommon; instead, defenses are strengthened, and experience is accumulated through steady, incremental work. Oyama's principles are embodied by cybersecurity specialists who remain up-to-date on the latest advancements, gradually hone their abilities, and improve security processes to successfully combat growing threats.

This idea is applicable to a wide range of fields and facets of human development. People who want to succeed in any field or career can benefit from adopting a mindset that emphasizes small, continuous growth, similar to a martial artist who improves their craft through constant practice and perfection. Success in learning a new language, mastering a technical skill, or improving physical fitness mostly depends on persistent effort and accumulating small victories.

Because of Oyama's wisdom, we should not only respect every advancement, no matter how small, but also enjoy the process of constant progress. It serves as a reminder that while development is sometimes quiet and modest, it is unwavering in its pursuit of mastery.

Adopting the 'little by little' mindset provides a sustainable route to success for anyone attempting to accomplish personal or professional objectives, as well as those navigating the challenges of cybersecurity. It reminds us that even if the objectives may seem far off, we are closer to reaching them with every step we take on the correct path. This kind of thinking builds perseverance, resilience, and a strong conviction that small victories added together will eventually result in significant and worthwhile accomplishments.

Essentially, Masutatsu Oyama's principle is a potent road map for long-term development and proficiency. It serves as a reminder that doing things one step at a time is not only a practical approach but also crucial when faced with difficult obstacles and lofty objectives. This method, characterized by consistent effort and gradual development, enables people to successfully navigate the challenges of their goals and achieve long-term success.

The just man is not one who does harm to none, but one whom having the power to harm represses the will.

Pythagoras

Pythagoras's insight into the nature of true justice — emphasizing restraint and moral discernment in those with the power to harm — speaks volumes about the ethical responsibilities that come with power. This theory transcends time and disciplinary boundaries, resonating particularly in the field of cybersecurity, where individuals often have significant control over digital spaces.

Pythagoras believed that the true measure of justice was not only avoiding committing crimes but also making the deliberate choice to utilize one's power for the good of others, particularly when that power could be used for evil. This is demonstrated in cybersecurity by experts who choose to act morally when they find flaws in systems, even those of rivals or enemies. They could exploit these flaws for their own benefit or to harm others. Instead, they choose to notify others about these vulnerabilities, ensuring they are fixed before being used maliciously.

This behavior demonstrates a thorough comprehension of the moral ramifications of one's skills and decisions. It emphasizes a dedication to the greater good above self-interest or mere use of authority. By doing this, cybersecurity professionals exemplify the Pythagorean just person; they show great moral bravery and a commitment to maintaining the integrity and security of digital spaces for everyone.

Furthermore, this concept promotes a reflective attitude toward power, asking those who possess the ability to shape or modify the digital environment to consider the wider consequences of their choices. It is a call to action to prioritize ethical issues over individual or corporate goals, creating a digital ecosystem based on mutual respect, accountability, and trust.

The insights of Pythagoras also convey a more general message about the nature of justice and the place of the individual in any society, whether it be online or elsewhere. It implies that real justice is attained by actively choosing to do good, particularly when there is a chance to do otherwise, rather than merely by the lack of malice. This viewpoint promotes proactive approaches to ethical conduct, including deterrents to harm and constructive contributions to the community.

In summary, Pythagoras' maxim enhances our comprehension of justice and serves as a model for moral behavior in cybersecurity and other fields. It serves as a reminder that the real test of a person's justice and integrity is found in how they choose to use their authority, particularly in situations when they have the chance to harm others. People can make a big difference in building a safer, fairer, and more ethical society by suppressing the urge to harm and instead acting with integrity and ethical responsibility.

The true warrior ponders the future without discarding the past while living in the present.

F. J. Chu

F. J. Chu skillfully explains the fundamental equilibrium that a true warrior must maintain in his perceptive remark on the core of a warrior's mindset: a harmonious combination of reverence for the past, readiness for the future, and acute awareness of the present. This mindset, which parallels the tactical methodology of an experienced cybersecurity specialist, acts as a foundational idea for attaining balance in every aspect of one's life.

Like a cybersecurity specialist, a true warrior explores the past not only for self-reflection but also for gaining insightful knowledge. A warrior learns from previous battles and approaches, just as a cybersecurity expert examines prior attacks and weaknesses to improve defenses. This retrospective examination is essential for strengthening their commitment and honing their abilities, better equipping them to face future challenges.

Cybersecurity professionals must be vigilant for new threats and continually adapt to them. To stay one step ahead of potential adversaries, they carefully forecast possible attack routes. This proactive mindset is necessary to foresee and neutralize new threats and quickly adjust to rapid advancements in hacking techniques.

However, the capacity to stay grounded in the present is what truly defines a cybersecurity warrior. They excel in instantaneous, real-time network activity monitoring, even amidst the ongoing assessment of past experiences and potential futures. Their keen attention to detail allows them to quickly recognize and eliminate imminent threats, embodying the essence of a warrior who is fully present in the moment.

F. J. Chu's portrayal of the wisdom of the true warrior provides a comprehensive foundation for cybersecurity strategy. It emphasizes combining past knowledge, readiness for the future, and awareness of the present to create a robust defensive system. By embracing the mindset of a true cybersecurity warrior—learning from past data, being prepared for upcoming challenges, and remaining vigilant—we can strengthen our digital infrastructures against the dynamic and ever-evolving world of cyber threats. This approach demonstrates the age-old wisdom of striking a balance between the past, present, and future in the pursuit of excellence while ensuring a secure digital environment.

Trained fighters, much more than average people, have an obligation to employ their skills judiciously. To govern themselves and their emotions at all times.

Peter Hobert

Peter Hobert skillfully captures the idea of accountability and restraint among skilled combatants in this fascinating piece of warrior wisdom. It highlights that persons with specific combat capabilities have a higher responsibility to use caution and judgment when employing those skills.

The insight highlights the higher bar skilled combatants maintain for their deeds and choices. They are not just regular people; they have special powers that necessitate exercising greater responsibility when using their abilities.

This warrior wisdom strongly emphasizes the necessity of maintaining constant self-control over one's emotions. Combat professionals are exhorted to maintain composure and control over their emotions even when confronted with difficult or emotionally taxing circumstances. By doing this, individuals exhibit actual mastery of their skills and show that they can make morally righteous decisions.

This knowledge serves to remind skilled combatants that their abilities have the potential for both good and bad. They have a moral obligation to use their abilities wisely, employing force only when it is absolutely essential to defend themselves or others.

This warrior wisdom is particularly applicable to ethically educated hackers, often known as "white hat" hackers or cybersecurity experts with specific knowledge in penetration testing and vulnerability assessments. Ethical hackers have a grave responsibility to use their abilities wisely. Instead of utilizing their knowledge to harm or exploit vulnerable systems, they use it to find and fix security flaws in organizational networks.

By adhering to strict rules and codes of behavior, these ethical hackers ensure their actions are consistent with moral values and legal restrictions. They conduct authorized and controlled penetration testing to identify potential weaknesses and help organizations enhance security defenses.

Ethical hackers exhibit a high degree of professionalism and integrity by maintaining self-control and emotional discipline at all times. They practice restraint, refraining from exploiting their abilities for wrongdoing or personal gain.

Ethical hackers are also morally obligated to collaborate with organizations to strengthen their cybersecurity posture and responsibly report their findings. They play a crucial role in preserving user privacy, safeguarding sensitive data, and creating a safer online environment.

Ethically trained hackers can lead by example in ethical cybersecurity practices by adopting this warrior knowledge. Their commitment to applying their expertise for the benefit of society fosters a climate of trust and cooperation among cybersecurity professionals and enhances the overall security of digital infrastructure.

By embracing this warrior wisdom, we can promote a culture of accountability and moral behavior, where individuals with specialized skills recognize the significance of their capabilities and strive to protect peace, justice, and the welfare of others.

The first law of war is to preserve ourselves and destroy the enemy.

Mao Tse-Tung

The declaration made by Mao Tse-Tung, "The first law of war is to preserve ourselves and destroy the enemy," provides a sobering but crucial understanding of the mechanics of battle. Fundamentally, this axiom emphasizes the main goal of every conflict: defending oneself while neutralizing the harm posed by the adversary. This well-worn tactic has a powerful resonance in the field of cybersecurity, serving as a constant reminder of the critical need for defense while actively reducing risks.

Today's digital environment is like a contemporary battlefield, with a wide range of cyber threats continuously encircling individuals and companies. These threats might take the form of sophisticated phishing attacks designed to deceive or harmful software like viruses, trojans, worms, and ransomware. Mao's insight in this regard points to a two-pronged strategy.

First and foremost, self-preservation highlights the necessity of strong cybersecurity safeguards. This entails setting up firewalls, frequently updating software, and monitoring for any emerging threats. It translates to using strong passwords, being wary of unsolicited contacts, and routinely backing up important data as part of basic cyber hygiene. Together, these precautions serve as fortifications, protecting valuable data assets and maintaining system integrity.

Second, in the context of cyberspace, the directive to "destroy the enemy" refers to preemptive actions meant to detect, neutralize, and eradicate threats. This entails acquiring threat intelligence, understanding the tactics of potential attackers, and proactively reducing vulnerabilities that could be exploited—rather than conducting retaliatory cyberattacks. Organizations can detect and stop assaults before they happen by staying one step ahead and understanding their enemy, in this case, cybercriminals and their tools, tactics, and techniques (TTPs).

Philosophically speaking, Mao's instruction also serves as a reminder of the stakes. Data breaches and cyberattacks can cause serious operational, reputational, and financial harm in today's world. The necessity and value of self-preservation and the need to neutralize threats cannot be overstated.

Even though Mao Tse-Tung made these statements in a different era, their applicability in the modern digital age is undeniable. His wisdom serves as a beacon as we navigate the complex web of digital threats, reminding us to prioritize our defense and always stay alert to ward off any potential dangers.

The more you sweat in training, the less you bleed in battle.

Navy Seal Maxim

The Navy SEAL saying, "The more you sweat in training, the less you bleed in battle," encapsulates the essence of readiness and underscores the importance of rigorous training for a warrior. This traditional wisdom demonstrates that the effort and intensity put into preparation directly impact performance in real-world scenarios. It teaches that true victories, whether in the military or other fields, are often secured through extensive training and practice long before the actual battle.

The warrior way of life, characterized by discipline, toughness, and commitment, exemplifies this saying. It's not enough to know how to fight; continual improvement and skill development are essential. A warrior's training is not just a means to prepare for battle; it becomes an integral part of their identity. This rigorous training ensures that when a warrior faces challenges, their response is almost instinctual, the result of years of practice and effort. The less you need to think, the quicker your reactions, and the more ingrained your strategies are, the higher your chances of success.

This concept is highly relevant in cybersecurity, especially in "red team" and "blue team" drills. In these simulations, the "red team" acts as attackers trying to exploit system vulnerabilities. In contrast, the "blue team" works to detect and stop these threats. Like a warrior's rigorous training, these exercises provide cybersecurity professionals with a safe environment to practice their skills, anticipate potential threats, and enhance defenses.

By "sweating" in these simulated cyber battlegrounds, professionals ensure that when a real threat arises, they possess not only the technical skills to address it but also the experience of having faced similar challenges before. Although the preparation is demanding and time-consuming, it reduces the "bleeding" or damage caused by an actual cybersecurity breach. It teaches professionals to think on their feet, adapt quickly, and respond to threats with precision, akin to a seasoned soldier on the battlefield.

Ultimately, the Navy SEAL maxim serves as a continual reminder of the significance of preparedness, adherence to protocols, and perseverance—all essential components of the warrior's code. Warriors have known for centuries, and cybersecurity experts recognize today that success stems from consistent training and dedication. On the battlefield or in the virtual world, the sweat and hard work of training safeguard against real-world challenges.

But here we may wonder what he would do if nobody knew anything about it.

The Code of the Samurai

"The Code of the Samurai" asks us to consider what integrity truly means, especially in situations with little public recognition or scrutiny. It challenges us to reflect deeply on the nature of our invisible acts and consider whether our actions align with our stated beliefs and ideals, even without outside approval.

This thoughtful question explores the essence of moral conduct by suggesting that genuine virtue involves upholding honor not only while behaving morally in public but also when no one else is around. It emphasizes the significance of following one's moral compass and exercising self-guidance, independent of social praise or reward, referring to the inner drive that propels our decisions.

This idea becomes especially relevant in the context of cybersecurity. Consider the ethical hacker who, upon identifying a serious vulnerability, decides to quietly disclose it to protect the wider integrity of the digital ecosystem as well as the immediate interests of the impacted party. Their deed, performed without anticipating recognition, embodies the ideal of honesty as stated in "The Code of the Samurai." The choices that go unspoken and outside the spotlight truly determine a professional's ethical standing.

The quote from "The Code of the Samurai" is a potent mirror, revealing our actual character through our deeds that others cannot see. It emphasizes the value of moral alignment within oneself over external validation and promotes living a life where one's actions are always guided by a steadfast adherence to moral standards.

Ultimately, the wisdom in "The Code of the Samurai" urges us to live lives of silent integrity, where all we do consistently aligns with our highest principles, regardless of what others may think or acknowledge. Applied across disciplines, this ethos fosters an environment where ethical behavior is not just an outward performance but a reflection of our true selves. From the silent guardians of cybersecurity to the myriad other roles we play in life, it cultivates a foundation of trust, respect, and genuine character.

The angry man will defeat himself in battle as in life.

Samurai Maxim

The Samurai proverb, "The angry man will defeat himself in battle as in life," emphasizes how destructive anger can be and how it may be one's deadliest opponent in all undertakings. This wisdom extends beyond the battlefield, providing insightful guidance on career advancement, personal development, and conflict resolution in various contexts, including the complex area of cybersecurity.

This adage highlights how anger affects judgment, hinders strategic thinking, and can cause rash decisions that jeopardize goals and well-being. The tendency to react angrily to a breach or assault can be especially harmful in the context of cybersecurity, where threats are complex, and pressure is high. An impulsive reaction may overlook important information, misinterpret the threat's origin, or implement the wrong countermeasure, exacerbating the vulnerability rather than mitigating it.

This idea also emphasizes the value of emotional intelligence in effective management and leadership. Anyone in a position of authority, including cybersecurity professionals, must learn how to control their temper and channel their anger into focused concentration. This requires a thorough awareness of one's feelings, the self-control to refrain from acting on them impulsively, and the discernment to direct emotional energy into deliberate, productive action.

This Samurai proverb also generally relates to challenges in personal relationships and interactions with others. The capacity to control one's emotions and act with composure and clarity is essential when handling conflicts at work, personal struggles, or competition with others. It facilitates deliberate decision-making, builds resilience, and enhances one's ability to overcome challenges gracefully and efficiently.

Essentially, this adage tells us that our ability to manage our emotions often determines our level of success in both life and combat. By acknowledging the futility of anger and learning to manage our emotional responses effectively, we empower ourselves to act with intention and precision. This approach not only helps us navigate the complexities of cybersecurity but also improves our relationships and personal lives, guiding us toward more fruitful and satisfying outcomes.

In God we trust, the rest we polygraph.

FBI Agent Maxim

The agents' maxim of the Federal Bureau of Investigation (FBI), "In God we trust, the rest we polygraph," encapsulates a foundational principle in security and intelligence fields: "Trust but verify." Although this attitude might seem harsh, strict checks and balances are essential in high-stakes situations where a breach or betrayal could have disastrous results. This approach to trust is crucial not only for elite intelligence organizations but also for cybersecurity units, particularly those in a Security Operations Center (SOC) responsible for protecting an organization's most private data.

At its core, the FBI agent maxim stresses the need for constant monitoring and careful screening. While trust is important and necessary for teamwork, it cannot be blind. This principle is evident in the use of polygraphs or lie detector exams. In high-security situations, where the honesty and loyalty of staff can determine the success or compromise of an operation, tools like the polygraph provide an additional layer of verification to ensure individuals remain true to their oaths.

In terms of cybersecurity, the SOC serves as the nerve center of a company's digital defense system. SOC personnel have access to information about vital infrastructure, vulnerabilities, and sensitive data. Companies must exercise the same level of caution when hiring and retaining SOC staff as the FBI does when verifying the trustworthiness of its agents.

For cyber defense, this means that SOC workers must undergo thorough screening. Comprehensive background checks, frequent security training, and periodic re-evaluations are all crucial—even if polygraphs might not be the most practical tool. These procedures ensure that individuals responsible for safeguarding a business's digital assets possess not only the necessary technical expertise but also align socially and ethically with the organization's security objectives.

Insider threats are becoming an increasingly significant concern in the evolving field of cybersecurity, making the phrase "trust but verify" even more vital. An insider with malicious intent could wreak havoc using their extensive knowledge of the system. By maintaining stringent screening and monitoring procedures, businesses can mitigate these risks and ensure that their SOC remains a strong point of defense rather than a potential vulnerability.

This traditional proverb from FBI agents is a universal reminder of the thin line separating confidence from caution. While trust is crucial, verification ensures its accuracy. This holds true whether you're in the bustling centers of cybersecurity operations or the sacred corridors of national intelligence agencies.

Anger breeds confusion. To be clear-minded, you must avoid being angry.

The Bhagavad Gita

The Bhagavad Gita provides insightful knowledge on the relationship between mental clarity, confusion, and fury. It states clearly that anger impairs judgment and prevents people from making wise decisions and that avoiding anger is necessary to keep one's mind clear.

This wise counsel illustrates how anger disrupts thought processes. It shows how feelings like rage not only make it difficult to think clearly but also cause confusion, making it harder to make decisions. This knowledge is essential, especially in circumstances that require calm reasoning and poise.

This advice aligns with the warrior philosophy's emphasis on mental discipline and emotional control. Warriors and those who value this wisdom agree that it's critical to maintain mental clarity, particularly under challenging situations. For strategic thought and effective action, a clear mind is essential.

Applying this idea to the field of cybersecurity, imagine an incident that leads to great frustration and anger within the incident response team. These emotions may hinder clear communication, swift action, and proper issue resolution. However, by prioritizing mental discipline, the team can collaborate more effectively and reason clearly, enhancing their problem-solving abilities.

This cybersecurity scenario underscores the concept that succumbing to anger impedes clear thinking and fosters confusion. Emotional turmoil can seriously impair rational thought, as The Bhagavad Gita suggests. The incident response team's experience highlights the importance of emotional control in maintaining focus and effectively resolving issues.

In the end, this wisdom offers an insightful lesson in controlling emotions and their impact on critical thinking. Gaining emotional control and preserving mental clarity is crucial for making wise choices, addressing issues, and achieving goals in both personal and professional contexts, such as cybersecurity. This perspective promotes emotional intelligence and awareness, helping us approach problems and make decisions with balance.

Look well into thyself; there is a source of strength which will always spring up if thou wilt always look.

Marcus Aurelius

The great Roman Emperor and Stoic philosopher Marcus Aurelius imparted a wise insight that endures across time and cultural boundaries: "Look well within yourself; there is a source of strength which will always spring up if thou wilt always look." This advice, which emphasizes self-reflection and finding inner strength, is especially pertinent in the fast-paced world of cybersecurity. It underscores the importance of ongoing personal development and self-awareness as the cornerstones of resilience and success.

Professionals dealing with cybersecurity face a wide range of challenges in this dynamic field, including new and emerging cyber threats, rapid technological advances, and complex regulatory environments. Aurelius's insight suggests that despite these external pressures, looking inward can provide a source of resilience and fortitude. Cybersecurity professionals can confidently navigate their career paths by engaging in introspection, which promotes both personal and professional growth.

Self-reflection enables cybersecurity professionals to evaluate themselves honestly, identify their strengths, and pinpoint areas that need development. In a field where vulnerability equates to stagnation, this approach is essential. For example, an expert skilled in risk assessment might reflect on their work and realize they need to learn more about emerging sectors such as artificial intelligence, penetration testing, or cloud security. Recognizing these deficiencies encourages the pursuit of further education, ensuring their knowledge base remains current and comprehensive.

Furthermore, reflection is a valuable tool for navigating the ethical issues that arise in cybersecurity. Practitioners must often balance privacy concerns with security imperatives, requiring technical expertise and moral clarity. Frequent self-evaluation ensures their decisions align with ethical standards and social norms, protecting system integrity and individual rights.

Introspection also fosters a mindset conducive to creativity and strategic vision. Cybersecurity is not just about thwarting current threats but also about anticipating future challenges. Reflecting on past experiences—both positive and negative—yields important insights that inspire innovative thinking and well-considered planning.

Cybersecurity professionals can follow a path characterized by ongoing learning, moral integrity, and creative problem-solving by adhering to Marcus Aurelius's advice to seek inner strength through self-reflection. Drawing on one's inner reserves of strength and knowledge is essential in an environment where change and uncertainty are the norm. Frequent self-reflection not only enhances technical proficiency but also reaffirms a commitment to maintaining the highest levels of accountability and vision in safeguarding the digital domain.

Do, or do not. There is no try.

Yoda

The wise and formidable Jedi Master Yoda from the Star Wars trilogy famously said, "Do or do not. There is no try." This quote captures the spirit of will and dedication inherent to the warrior's way of life. It emphasizes the value of giving one's all to one's endeavors, whether in combat or any other activity. This advice is applicable to experts in the field of cybersecurity as well as individuals training to become masters in martial arts.

The path of the warrior is one of unrelenting dedication and willpower. A lack of resolve or heart can result in failure or, in the worst case, disastrous outcomes. Yoda's teachings serve as a reminder that one must fully commit to the course of action and see it through to completion when faced with adversities. Half-measures and indecision are not acceptable. This mindset is especially important in the field of cyber protection, where the stakes are high.

"Do or do not" is a principle in cybersecurity. The phrase "There is no try" reflects the necessity of taking a proactive and dedicated approach to protecting digital assets. Businesses must 'do' everything in their power to ensure the security of their networks and data, not just 'attempt' to do so. This entails implementing a thorough security plan that incorporates multiple layers of protection, including firewalls, intrusion detection systems, and encryption, as well as consistent staff training and awareness campaigns.

The idea of "defense in depth" is one important cyber defense principle that aligns with Yoda's wisdom. This technique involves using several tiers of security to ward off cyberattacks. Organizations must be fully committed to implementing a comprehensive security strategy, just as a warrior must be fully committed to their plan of action. It is not sufficient to simply 'attempt' to defend their network with a single layer of protection; organizations must 'do' everything in their power to safeguard their digital assets by implementing multiple levels of security measures.

Finally, Yoda's famous saying, "Do or do not. There is no try," is a poignant reminder of the value of dedication and resolve in all undertakings. This advice is especially pertinent to the world of cyber defense, where safeguarding digital assets requires a proactive and dedicated approach. In cybersecurity, this translates to fully committing to robust defense strategies and not merely attempting half-measures. By adopting this perspective and executing an all-encompassing, multi-tiered security plan, institutions can enhance their defenses against the diverse array of cyber hazards encountered in the contemporary digital terrain.

There is a best way to perform any task.

Bruce Lee

"There is a best way to perform any task" is a profound insight from Bruce Lee that speaks to the core of brilliance and mastery. It emphasizes the significance of dedication, unwavering perseverance, and continuous improvement to reach the highest level of success in any undertaking. This concept, rooted in martial arts, extends well beyond the mat, offering insightful advice on personal growth, career success, and the strategic execution of duties.

Lee's insight promotes a mindset of continuous development and a dedication to identifying the most efficient techniques. It encourages people to critically evaluate their methods, embrace creativity, and never stop seeking improvements. This search for the "best way" is not limited to combat; it applies to life's ethical and intellectual aspects, advocating for a comprehensive professional and personal development strategy.

This idea has strong applicability in the field of cybersecurity with the concept of "security by design." This method emphasizes incorporating security measures early in the development process to ensure that defenses are fundamental rather than added later. It mirrors Lee's call for effectiveness and planning, stressing the need to anticipate potential risks and take proactive measures to defend against them.

The idea of "security by design" reflects the readiness and strategic vision of the warrior. Cybersecurity specialists need to anticipate vulnerabilities and design systems that inherently mitigate these risks, just as a martial artist predicts an opponent's actions and counters them efficiently. This proactive strategy requires a thorough understanding of potential risks, creative problem-solving techniques, and a commitment to ongoing learning and adaptation.

Bruce Lee's timeless advice is to always seek the best way to complete a task, which is guidance for anyone following the warrior path, whether in cybersecurity, martial arts, or any other field requiring excellence. It promotes the notion that mastery of one's craft, strategic planning, and the relentless pursuit of progress are the keys to success, not complacency.

By adopting Lee's perspective, we are reminded that all actions, no matter how basic or complex, have the potential for improvement. By approaching our tasks with this mentality, we not only enhance our own capabilities but also advance our industries and embody the true spirit of a warrior who strives to exceed rather than merely achieve. This dedication to identifying and refining the most efficient approach ensures that we remain at the forefront of innovation and productivity, honoring the legacy that Bruce Lee personified.

A man's word is his honor.

Okinawan Proverb

The fundamental idea that one's integrity and reputation are strongly related to the commitments one makes and the truth one expresses is captured by the Okinawan adage, "A man's word is his honor." This insight emphasizes the importance of keeping one's word and underscores the significance of every spoken commitment. In a society where deceit and manipulation can prevail, this proverb advocates for a return to principles that value honesty, intention, and integrity.

This idea plays a crucial role in the field of cybersecurity. Consider a situation where a company representative guarantees clients their personal information is completely secure and guarded against breaches. However, soon after, a significant data breach occurs, exposing private data. In this instance, the organization's reputation is at risk not only because of the breach itself but also because of the discrepancy between their statements and actions.

Here, the idea of honor is immediately relevant. In the field of cybersecurity, keeping one's word demonstrates an organization's dedication to protecting user data as a matter of professional integrity. Serious repercussions, such as diminished customer confidence, legal penalties, and reputational harm to the company, may follow from breaking promises. This illustrates how keeping one's word affects an organization's credibility and accountability, going beyond simple rhetoric.

This military wisdom has broader implications that apply to many facets of life. It encourages us to be mindful of our speech and to reflect on our motivations. In addition to individual actions, keeping our promises and communicating honestly help to foster a culture of trust and integrity within groups. This insight prompts us to consider the motivation and intent behind our words and deeds, creating a deeper understanding of honor.

In the end, the proverb's lesson serves as a timeless reminder of the need for honesty in both our personal and professional interactions. Maintaining our word is not only a sign of our moral character but also a testament to the values and ideals that guide our behavior.

Don't appear just; be just.

Aechylus

"Don't appear just; be just" is a timeless warning from Aeschylus that powerfully advocates for moral integrity and sincerity. This age-old wisdom emphasizes the importance of truly embodying justice rather than merely performing acts of virtue. It urges us to live up to our moral convictions and highlights that true character is shown through actions, not appearances.

This concept is particularly significant in the field of cybersecurity, where experts are tasked with protecting confidential data. The real test of a cybersecurity expert's integrity is not in their pretenses of diligence or assurances of security given to clients but in their unwavering dedication to the strict implementation of security procedures, regular software updates, and the constant identification and mitigation of vulnerabilities. In cybersecurity, genuine justice is demonstrated through diligence and often overlooked effort.

Aeschylus's wisdom extends beyond cybersecurity and touches every facet of life. It reminds us that real virtue is the ability to live up to our principles even in the face of challenges. This dedication to true justice maintains our moral fiber, shapes our interpersonal and professional relationships, and fosters a culture of mutual respect and trust.

This proverb also encourages us to consider our actions in light of our moral compass. It challenges us to evaluate whether our deeds genuinely reflect our beliefs, not just how they appear to others. We foster an honest and accountable society when we prioritize ethical behavior over the appearance of integrity.

Aeschylus's maxim, "Don't appear just; be just," essentially serves as a core ethos for acting honorably and authentically in our interactions with others. It compels us to strive for true justice in all spheres of our existence, from safeguarding virtual spaces to navigating interpersonal relationships. We make a meaningful difference in a society that values honesty, morality, and genuine virtue when we live out justice rather than simply pretending to. A life well-lived is characterized by the pursuit of genuine justice, which is grounded in action and permeates both personal and professional endeavor

> "A journey of a thousand miles begins with a single step."
>
> Lao Tzu

www.ingramcontent.com/pod-product-compliance
Lightning Source LLC
Chambersburg PA
CBHW052258220526
45471CB00001B/393